Best Little Dance Hall

By 9 a.m., Mary's secret life has begun. Her three children are off to school, her husband is safely at work. Quickly she changes into black pants and a low-cut blouse (the one with the sparkly gold threads) and tries to coax her bleached blond hair to look like Farrah Fawcett's. Then she climbs into her green station wagon and makes a beeline for the Palms Danceland. Craftily, Mary parks out of sight, in the back lot. "My husband followed me here one day, and boy, did that cause a ruckus," she remembers sourly. "I guess he thinks I don't come here anymore, but he'd have to be some kind of fool to believe that."

Mary is one of several hundred patrons who mark time—and in some cases, make time—at the Palms Danceland, a Dallas hangout for bored housewives who are outnumbered only by wandering husbands. The Palms, and places like it, are a Texas tradition, though they are cropping up elsewhere. Open for business from 9 to 3, they used to be dubbed "pressure cooker" clubs; now they're called "microwave" clubs, in homage to the kitchen aids that free matrons to dance the day away and still have supper ready when their husbands drag in from work. "Sure he'd like me to sit home in a rocking chair all day watching the soap operas," says Mary grudgingly. "I'd just wither and die if I had to do that. I like to dance too much."

Texas Waltz: The Palms country-and-western band is already bleating "Together Again," and couples are dancing the Texas waltz, in which men put their arms around the women's shoulders and the women hook their fingers through the men's belt loops. "May I have the pleasure of this dance?" a middle-aged man named Roy asks Mary. "You certainly may," she declares. Roy, it turns out, is a carpenter who has the day off due to bad weather, and, as he tells it, "There ain't nothing to go home for." Also on hand are shift workers, off-duty firemen, construction workers and one man who informs his dance partner, "I'm a crook." Nearby, a truck salesman in a three-piece suit tries out his favorite pickup line: "You ever do the Y-dance?" "No," comes the reply, "what's that?" The man stops dancing, grins and says, "Why dance?"

At one of the green Formica tables sits the expensively dressed wife of an entertainment promoter, who arrives every day in her shiny Cadillac—and always leaves alone. Like other "unescorted ladies," she escapes the $1.50 cover charge and gets free beer as long as she is not sitting with a man. A debonair man in his early 60s and a middle-aged woman in a

Photos by Shelly Katz—Black Star

Owner Taylor at the Palms: Bored housewives, wandering husbands

bouffant hair-do also show up every day. "It's no secret that we've been meeting here for four years," he says. "I'm married and so is she, but we're real close," he adds politely.

An unofficial code of conduct exists at the Palms. It's first names only and marital status is rarely discussed, though everyone seems to know the score. "The women always say they're in the process of getting a divorce," says the truck salesman. "But they'd do better if they said they were married." "Sure the men are all married," sniffs Barbara Meyers, a pretty brunette who says *her* divorce is almost final. "Otherwise they wouldn't come to this place. Me, I come 'cause I like to dance, but a lot of men aren't satisfied with that. They want you to leave with them," she says indignantly.

Apparently, there are dictates about this, too. After one dance, a man will graciously return his partner to her table. After a second or third, his hands tend to get a bit friendly. But serious propositions come only when the woman seems responsive. For those who do respond, several nearby motels offer special day rates, part of the support industry that has bloomed around the Palms. Don and Carlene Taylor, who own the club, get their customers a 10 per cent discount at the day-care center down the road.

Telltale Odors: Since most patrons are married, but not to each other, some customers go to extraordinary lengths not to be found out. One day, Taylor was working on the roof when he spotted a woman in the parking lot frantically wriggling out of her housedress and into party clothes. One housewife always leaves by 2:30 so she has time to wash telltale smoke odors from her hair. Another waits for her husband to go on his Sunday fishing trips, then madly whips up seven dinners and hides them in the freezer.

As further precaution, the Palms is kept so dark that it takes a newcomer a full ten minutes to see anything, enough time for an errant spouse to beat a hasty retreat. One man ran into his wife in the club recently—for the second time. "They were both pretty embarrassed," recalls Don Taylor. "But they didn't make a scene. They talked for a while, then left."

Soap Opera: Though Carlene doesn't deny that some serious hanky-panky transpires, she also believes one of the Palms's attractions is that "people can tell their life stories here and not be afraid." In fact, the place sometimes sounds like the set of a live soap opera. "I lived with a man for 24 weeks," says Millie, 45, a divorcee with three children. "I've never gotten over him. Now, I live with a man from Louisiana who travels." She points to a pudgy woman in a red pantsuit. "That's my sister. She's married to a man who's studying for the ministry. He's sworn off relations until he finishes studying the Bible." She motions to another woman. "Her husband runs around on her. And that woman next to her caught her husband fooling around with his nephews. See that woman? She was in love with that guy across the room. Got pregnant by him, but he didn't do right by her."

Understandably, Taylor is sensitive to the charge that his club ruins marriages. "We probably save ten marriages for every one that breaks up," he insists. "They wouldn't be running around if it weren't already on the rocks. This is the only thing holding it together." Still, Taylor knows that too much of a good thing is not good for business, which is why he closes promptly at 3. "It's kind of like ice cream," he says. "You eat as much of it as you want and you get sick of it. This way they just want to come back for more."

—DIANE K. SHAH with LEA DONOSKY in Dallas

JUST COUNTRY

JUST COUNTRY

Country People, Stories, Music

Robert Cornfield
with
Marshall Fallwell, Jr.

McGraw-Hill Book Company

New York   St. Louis   San Francisco
Düsseldorf   Mexico   Toronto

Book design by Ivan Paslavsky.

1 2 3 4 5 6 7 8 9 R A B P 7 9 8 7 6

Library of Congress Cataloging in Publication Data

Cornfield, Robert.
Just country: country people, stories, music.

1.   Country music—United States—History and
criticism.   I.   Fallwell, Marshall, joint author.
II.   Title.
ML3561.C69C67   784   76-17061
ISBN 0-07-013184-8
ISBN 0-07-013178-3 pbk.

4

For Jaqueline and Chris

Acknowledgments

Though the compiling and writing of this book was a collaborative effort at all points, Marshall Fallwell and I believe some indication of particular responsibility should be noted. All photographs except where otherwise credited are by Marshall Fallwell, and he wrote chapters six and nine.

My personal thanks go to Barbara John for early encouragement and direction, Dale Harris, Luigia Norsa, Les Leverett, and Jo Walker and Betty Young of the Country Music Association. Marshall extends his thanks to Bill Henderson, David Harscheid, Bruno Monkus, and John Gabree. Together, Marshall and I are delighted to acknowledge our gratitude to our patient, insightful, and enthusiastic editor, Fred Hills. Bob Pinson of the Country Music Foundation Library and Media Center saved us from many blunders with his peerless knowledge of the subject. His generosity, as well as his scholarship, are known throughout the country music world.

We apologize to the hundreds of fine singers and writers and country music workers of all sorts whose names have not been included, and we hope they will forgive us and understand that we mean this book to pay tribute to a popular music art which all of us love.

Robert Cornfield

Foreword
by Minnie Pearl

Country music has been dealt with in more ways than I care to imagine, but this book is the most unique treatment of the subject I've come across.

Authors have a way of seeing country music objectively—and I suppose that has its virtues—but we performers see the whole scene as a family story. And I'm not too sure that's the truest way to view it, prejudiced as we all are by our personal feelings towards our brothers and sisters in the business.

Just Country is an ambitious, affectionate approach to country music. A great deal of research has been done and many areas are delved into as never before in other books. I am impressed, perhaps mainly because I have never thought about country music in this manner. I think readers will enjoy the book whether they are country music fans or not. It is an important historical treatment of an art form which is a part of Americana.

When I came on the scene in 1940, I was conscious of the fact that country music had a tendency to be segregated. Its fans were sort of separated from other music lovers. They fell into a category, then, of people primarily of country backgrounds who related to the music they had grown up with in rural areas.

Then I began to sense a wonderful change as the years went by. People from all walks of life were beginning to enjoy our music. So-called "city folks" started showing up at our concerts and personal appearances. We began to be booked into the "better" halls and auditoriums; I was with the group that played Carnegie Hall in 1947. We were becoming recognized as an accepted form of "general music," one which is now in the mainstream of the American tradition.

And we continued to grow. Network television put us in the homes of America, and the Opry, of course, continued on the radio. The life-styles of my fellow performers changed. They moved into beautiful homes and began to enjoy a touch of gracious living that few had known during the years they had been struggling "pickers." They flew to engagements or traveled in luxurious buses that made one-night stands more comfortable. Some of the performers changed as a result of this rich living, but the majority have remained the down-to-earth folks they were when they were just beginning.

I congratulate Robert Cornfield and Marshall Fallwell, Jr., on the truly fine job they have done. Every time a prestigious book like this reaches the stores, we performers are even more proud of our heritage. We are "just so proud to be here!"

Contents

George Jones.

1
Country
People

Country is not only a
variety of American popular music; it is a world and a way
of life. To meet all who live in that world is like coming to
a great gathering of a clan. To talk with them is to learn
of the old days and the hard times of grandparents and great-
grandparents, whispered tales of black sheep, tough times
now, tall stories and raucous jokes.

The family has spread all over the land, and it is
as varied as its members' dress; they wear cowboy outfits
and gingham dresses, slacks and Hawaiian shirts, jeans and
tight-fitting beaded dresses. Some of the relatives are hell-
raisers and boozers, religious fanatics or simply God-fearing,
devoted daddies and loyal moms. There is plenty of gossip
about, what with cheating wives, no-good children, drifters,
shady ladies with hearts of gold.

They've farmed, worked railroad gangs, been truckers
and mechanics, baseball players, machinists. Some of their
names are familiar words and fit together, like Cash and

Pride, Haggard and Rich, McCoy and Paycheck. Most names sound English: Anderson, Lynn, Tucker, Monroe, Acuff, Bailey, Macon, Rodgers. But before you start thinking the family is a little restricted, they'll point out a Rodriguez and a Friedman.

When you ask country performers what is so different and special about country, they tell you it is sincere, that it tells about real problems like work and love and death, and foolin' around and sex and divorce. Its language is simple, clear, and direct, without any of acid rock's symbolism and superfantasy or convolutions, nor popular music's flights of poetry ("fly me to the moon"), but since it is a music that blends many styles, it doesn't hesitate to borrow a few new ones. All it does is temper them down a bit and make them easier to take.

Country music began as folk music, and in fact that is what it still is today—our American national music. Its tradition is long and rich, though only within the last decade has it been given the acclaim that has been its due.

The first astounding fact about country is that it is essential to the most loyal of its audience. They cannot live without it, for it is their entire artistic expression, and for many it supplants or complements religion.

The close identification with music is perhaps the most glorious part of the Southern heritage of country, and such deep loyalty demonstrates itself with other Southern virtues: hospitality, sense of kinship, good will, family love, adherence to the ideal of a simple life.

Maybe it is this very sense of family that has kept country stars from becoming national celebrities. The audience doesn't want them to be distant. To say that Jimmie Rodgers

Bill Anderson.

is among the greatest popular entertainers this country has produced is as disconcerting as learning your cousin has been nominated for an Academy Award. Someone to whom you have felt so close, who sang his songs intimately to you, who is a part of yourself, can't be made to sound so grand. If he is some sort of genius, then you must be some sort of genius, and that just doesn't make sense.

Country audiences want their performers to get the respect due them, but they don't want them too high on a pedestal. They'll knock them down a peg if they get too swell— and the worst thing that could happen to a country performer is to "lose touch with his audience."

The performers know this well and they are always ready to talk with the folks who come to see their shows. In interviews they remind us continually of their humble beginnings, and how well they remember their struggles, how they really prefer to clean house, or fish, or laze around— in fact, they are lazy like the rest of us. The difference is that they feel a "mission" to perform because they owe it to their fans—and they are grateful to God for giving them their talent, which they have to be faithful to.

In country, it is better to be known as someone who occasionally slips around, raises hell, is prone to irrational acts of violence, has been through a few marriages, or has served time than to take on airs and act as if you were important. Not too long ago, there was a list of sell-outs— those who had a big-time television show and appearing on commercials, like Johnny Cash. When Eddy Arnold donned a tuxedo and became a night-club performer he, too, was called to task. Real country fans are suspicious of the likes of **Glen Campbell or John Denver or Kris Kristofferson or**

Loretta Lynn and Ernest Tubb. (Photo: Les Leverett)

Merle Haggard.

Bob Dylan because they "play up" to all audiences. The tension is great, for country performers want a broad audience, yet they fear offending the loyal country fans (the most loyal in the world) by giving in to the enemy (commercial popular music). Only one man has managed it all, and that is Elvis Presley. He is a mighty exception.

The traditionalists who have never recovered from the shock of rock-and-roll (which actually revitalized country music) now complain about the sweeping violins that back many a country singer on records. There is a debate whether the velvety tones of Bill Anderson and Charlie Rich can rightly be called country, even though both men have had long, successful careers. There are the problems of the bluegrass

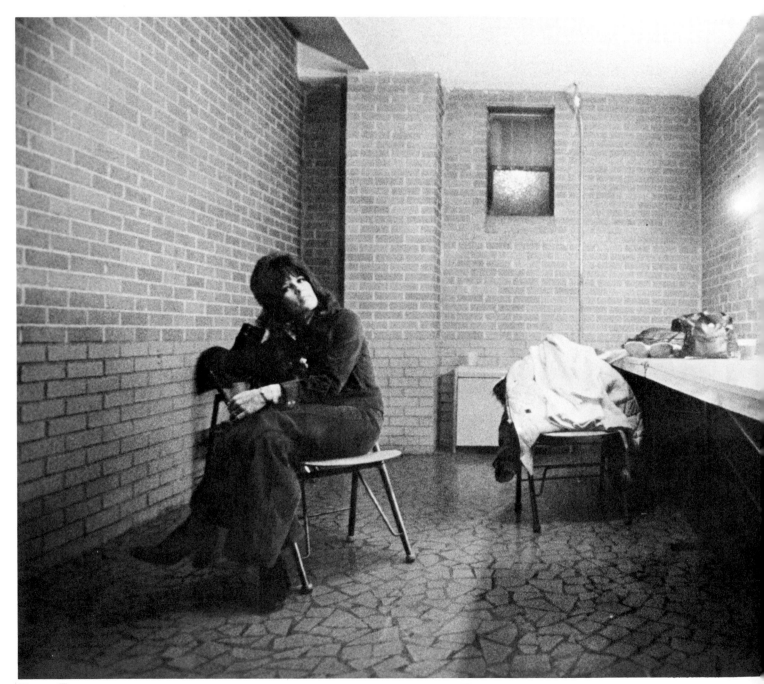

Donna Fargo.

turks, who are carrying musical invention too far along the road for comfort.

Yet, for all the hoopla about Nashville being the hub of a cold, impersonal, multimillion-dollar business, the real core of country music remains just folks and family.

Some of the new audience for country like to picture themselves as getting back to a pure expression of rural America. They feel as though they are returning to the land or they are moonshiners drunkenly lamenting or Saturday-night come-to-towners rowdying away. They got it wrong. It's a lot more complicated than that.

For years, country entertainers have carried on this hick act themselves, and by their sides have stood Western

Tammy Wynette.

Tammy Wynette.

Kris Kristofferson.

Dolly Parton.

dudes in fancy getups any right-minded horse would bolt at. Like all myths, it has an element of truth, but it is a blown-up self-parody that has misled too many Americans—television shows like "The Beverly Hillbillies" and "Petticoat Junction" thrived on this demeaning conception. The singers and instrumentalists hate it—and that is why they are either too dolled up or too casual. They want to be anything but hick. That self-made image has become a monster.

The paradox is that those who want to rid themselves of the hick image do everything to foster it. Basic country, it has been said, is a fiddle and a nasal twang. Half-joking, Tom T. Hall said, it is "playing the guitar and singing through my nose, which is what all country people who are in this business do. . . ." Also, it is a banjo, a mandolin, or a Hawaiian steel guitar. Nowadays, it is electric instruments made to copy those sounds.

Behind that image and misconceived notion, you can hear in today's songs the features of their ancestors—English and Scottish ballads, church hymns, gospel songs, a touch of Spanish-Mexican melody and rhythm, hoedowns and reels, French Cajun tunes, cowboy laments, Dixieland jazz, minstrel numbers, the blues.

Country has had many names—old-timey, hillbilly, mountain, Western—but whatever the name, you always knew what it was, and you certainly knew what it wasn't, like opera, or symphony or anything really slick and professional. The

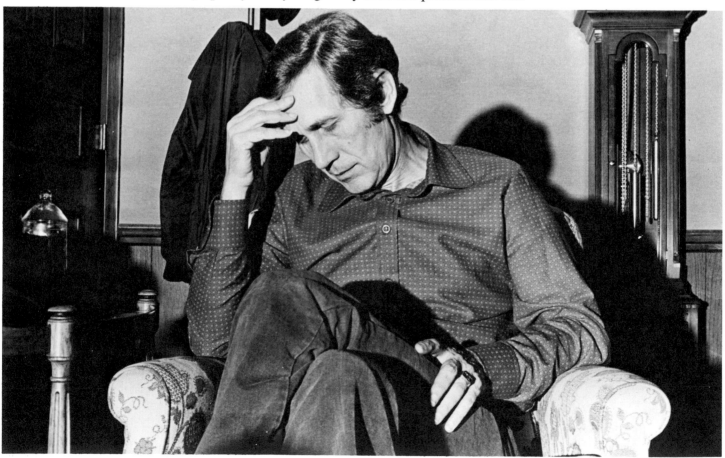
Chet Atkins.

18

Skeeter Davis.

Dottie West.

Skeeter Davis, Doug Kershaw, Dottie West.

19

important thing was always the way the song was sung, with a high nasal voice suggesting a whine but generally expressionless, and the instrumentation—a fiddle earliest on, then on to a banjo and a guitar.

The real clue is the word that occurs over and over again, *sincere*. It is music of the "folk" in that the musical impulse is kept simple and direct and disguises its ingenuity and inventiveness by keeping that sometimes extraordinary accomplishment and dexterity that great country artists have within the realm of the playful. Sometimes the very best country musicians are so self-effacing, like Bill Monroe and Bob Wills, that they seem to hide their genius.

In that way, country sticks close to its audience by

Charley Pride.

20

reassuring them that if they had the time, the guts, the chance, the added push, they, too, could be performers. The words of the songs are so idiomatic they seem pulled out of yesterday's conversation.

There is good reason all those people travel day and night to attend an Opry performance. There is good reason country performers have more personal-appearance dates and in more places than any other performers. The audience participation and response is so immediate and intense—there is so much identification—that for the audience it seems a chance for *them* to perform. That is the special gift country performers are given. In the form of the performer, the member of the audience steps on stage. That is the effect the country performer strives for. No wonder those outside the country family can't understand why some country artists are "great."

To experience the country magic, you have to go to a live performance, not merely to the star shows, but to see the small groups and the small-time performers who appear in roadhouses and taverns.

Charley Pride.

Many people feared that real country would die out because the popular singers were ignoring the heritage and diluting the country sound and voice to appeal to a broad-based audience. It didn't happen. The tradition continues, but time has made a difference. There are new singers for new audiences, and though the underlying themes remain the same they are presented with a modern sense of life: In 1946 the top country song was Merle Travis's "Divorce Me C.O.D.," a comic number, and in 1968 the top song was Tammy Wynette's "D-I-V-O-R-C-E," a word that couldn't be spoken in front of the children because that was precisely what the parents were going through.

Country is being invaded by foreigners too, specifically England's Olivia Newton-John and Canada's Anne Murray (though Hank Snow and Montana Slim also hailed from Canada). They *are* country, but like North Carolina's Ronnie Milsap, they want to avoid the tag—they want to leave themselves free.

When Milsap and Newton-John won the 1974 Country Music Awards, there was a cry of rage, and an ad hoc group was formed, including George Jones and Tammy Wynette, to establish another series of awards for "real" country performers. Because of such careful guardianship and caution, true country survives. It grows and changes along with the rest of the land that is its real home.

Country music is filled with the hankering to go back in time, to recover a lost period when things were sure and stable and uncomplicated. But more remarkable and less noticed is that country always manages to keep up with present issues and absorb new trends. Musically, it constantly reinvents and reinvigorates itself. As it turned out, rock-and-roll didn't destroy country; it shifted country's direction.

It is relatively easy to discuss the social reasons for country's staying power, but there is another reason too often overlooked, and that is its musical solidity and depth. Recently, the old string bands, the virtuosi of the fiddle, and the technical brilliance of bluegrass musicians like Bill Monroe have come to get their long overdue recognition.

There have not been many great voices in country (in fact, there are better voices around now than there ever were), but those old singers have perfect diction (regional though it might be) and a natural sense of phrasing, of giving the emotion of the song its clearest expression. Most country singers will tell you they never had a lesson in their lives, yet the incidence of singers with perfect pitch is more frequent

Arlene and Barbara Mandrell.

Arlene and Barbara Mandrell.

Barbara Mandrell.

23

Jerry Reed.

Glen Campbell.

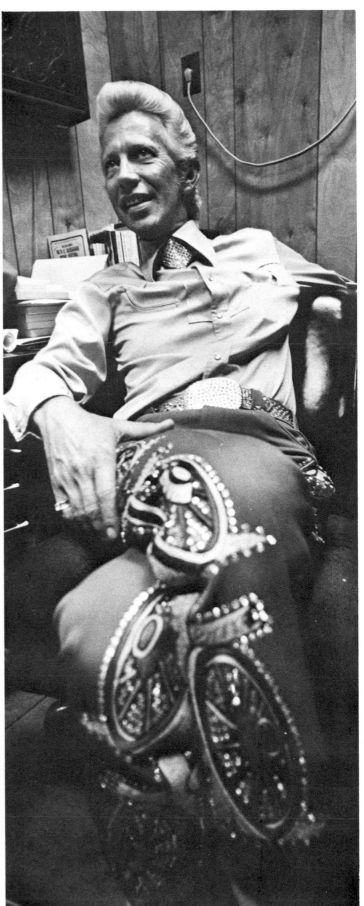

Porter Wagoner.

than in popular music—the vocal distortions of Liza Minelli or Barbra Streisand are unthinkable for country singers. You are more likely to hear sloppy singing at the Metropolitan Opera House than at the Grand Ole Opry. If anything, country suffers sometimes from a too clean and deadening perfection.

There is a whole group of country artists who are basically storytellers—Johnny Cash and Tom T. Hall are the most celebrated, but here, too, musical values are not ignored.

The stories are often autobiographical, and they tend to fall into self-pity and evasiveness. The "true" becomes fiction because it is made to conform to the values of the American way of life, and an American picture of existence. That so often the tales are sad is strange—lovers who drown

Lynn Anderson.

themselves in the brook or who are separated because one of them is in jail have been replaced by modern-day tragedies: divorce, a veteran trapped in a wheelchair while his wife slips out to fool around, a partner walking out, lovers who will leave in the morning and never come back.

It seems as though the anger and the disappointment are stronger than any that could be caused by the specific soap-opera situations of the songs. Real discontent is expressed with the whole of life—with your job and the government, the unclear social structure, unfulfilled ambitions, unfulfilled American dreams, constant insecurity, bitterness that you aren't among the winners. Put these feelings into a song, and the song turns out to be about spurned love.

Shel Silverstein.

Jeannie C. Riley and daughter Kim.

Melba Montgomery. (Courtesy William Morris Agency)

Bobby Bare.

Tanya Tucker.

Waylon Jennings.

Waylon Jennings.

This American music is our expression of our deepest feelings; and they are channeled into a steady beat, a clear set of phrases, and played on a guitar, banjo, and bass. It is a music that reflects both our idealism and our fears. It gave us native geniuses all of us should know more about—Jimmie Rodgers, the Carter Family, Bill Monroe, groups like Mainer's Mountaineers and Bob Wills and His Texas Playboys, master storytellers like Tom T. and Loretta Lynn, riveting personalities like Johnny Cash, and multifaceted musicians like Merle Haggard.

Of these we can be justly proud, for they told and still tell the story of this country, singing it loudly and clearly.

When you are around country people and country

Tammy Wynette.

singers you'll hear of working poor land that yielded almost nothing, sweating in textile mills and auto factories, lonely nights talking to your truck as if it were a woman, wanderers during the Depression years, prison terms and chain gangs and railroad gangs, of people called trash, hicks, crackers, hillbillies, Okies and Arkies, of rebellious children who pop pills, of the confusions of Vietnam and soldiers stationed in Germany drinking and fighting out of frustration.

What a wealth of living, what a storehouse of experience. That's what country music is.

Maybelle Carter.

2
Early
Country

I n the early twenties, the recording companies did not know what to call the music from the South. Their catalogues listed it under titles such as "Hill Country Tunes," "Old Familiar Tunes," "Songs of the Hills and Plains," "Old-time Music."

It took a while for companies to locate the audience for such music, and the pioneers who are credited with discovering country musicians and developing the market are honored in the annals of country as if they were artists themselves. The most celebrated scouts were Polk Brockman, Frank Walker, Art Satherley, Eli Oberstein, and Ralph Peer.

The man credited with the inspiration to record local talent is Polk Brockman, who in 1923 was the Atlanta distributor for Okeh records—a firm noted for its "race" records (black music for a black audience). On a trip to New York, Brockman saw a newsreel of country fiddlers at the Palace Theater and made a note to himself that someone should record a popular Georgia fiddler and moonshiner named Fiddlin' John Carson.

Within a month, Okeh sent down to Atlanta its recording director Ralph Peer with two engineers and, among other musicians, Fiddlin' John Carson was asked to make a disc. Carson's two songs were "The Old Hen Cackled and the Rooster's Going to Crow" and a popular song by Will Hays, written in 1871, "The Little Old Log Cabin in the Lane":

> The hinges they have rusted, the door is falling down
> The roof lets in the sunshine and the rain
> The only friend I've got now is this good old dog of mine
> In that little old log cabin in the lane.
>
> I ain't got long to stay here, what little time I've got
> I try to rest contented while I stay
> Until the day death calls me to find a better home
> Than this little old log cabin in the lane.

Peer thought Carson's songs and voice were awful, but the public ate it up, and by the end of the year, Peer realized that he had struck gold. Carson was brought to New York for more recordings, and the earlier recordings of old-time musicians like Henry Whitter and Eck Robertson which had been put to one side the year before were dusted off and given full commercial release.

It wasn't long before all the major recording companies got into the act, setting up Southern studios and making trips to ferret out talent.

These early recordings are now collector's items, and for some they represent the Golden Age of Country Music. The traditional sound was still clear, the performers energetic and sincere, the feel of authenticity in the music was supreme. All of today's country sounds and songs are derived from the classics of that time.

Some later recordings, still available, demonstrate what that music was like. The variety and accomplishment were already extraordinary. In Charlotte, North Carolina, Uncle Dave Macon, a vaudeville entertainer who became the first Grand Ole Opry star, recorded what is considered a country classic, "Cumberland Mountain Deer Race" which was based on an English poem, "The Wilde Ashe Deer." Macon makes it sound exactly like an English hunting song, his banjo creating the hunting peals and the rush and scramble.

The Dixon Brothers from Darlington County, South Carolina recorded "Down with the Old Canoe." That canoe's name was the *Titanic* and she was cut down in her pride by an iceberg because she was built by man and not by God. Its message was that man should always be prepared for death, for no one knows when Jesus Christ will take you. Today's country songs are close descendants, in lyric, theme and musical impulse, to this number and others like it.

Riley Puckett's and Gid Tanner's "On Tanner's Farm " is a "hard-luck" song, a type standard for country. It jokingly describes the plight of the tenant farmer, in this case a lazy gentleman who moves to a shack with cracks in the wall and no windows. Soon the pony is stolen and the merchant is looking for his pay. Tanner and Puckett were Georgia musicians and they joined with Clayton McMichen and Fate Norris to form the best, most imitated, and now classic string band, Gid Tanner and His Skillet Lickers.

The talent search was a strenuous and fascinating business. Art Satherley, who had come to this country from England in 1913, says he often clocked seventy thousand miles in forty-four weeks of traveling. For Satherley, the life he found in the South resembled the life he had left behind in England. The songs he heard on the roads and in churches were remarkably similar too. Satherley found his musicians in the fields, in factories, and in churches—and he recorded them in the back of trucks and in jails. Among his recording problems were dealing with washboards and cowbells and saws.

A. P. Carter.
(Courtesy Country Music Foundation Library and Media Center)

In 1930, Satherley was the first to record Gene Autry, and later went on to make the best of Bob Wills's records. His finds and those whose careers he also furthered include Roy Acuff, Red Foley, Bill Monroe, Ernest Tubb, and Eddy Arnold.

Usually, the record agents would advertise in the local papers and then select the best performers. Frank Walker of Columbia Records, the man responsible for the joining of Tanner and McMichen, would record in a local rented old building and decorate it to make the performers feel at home. He categorized the songs as gospel and religious, jigs and reels, sentimental songs, and "event" songs—the latter being those which told of famous events like the death of the miner

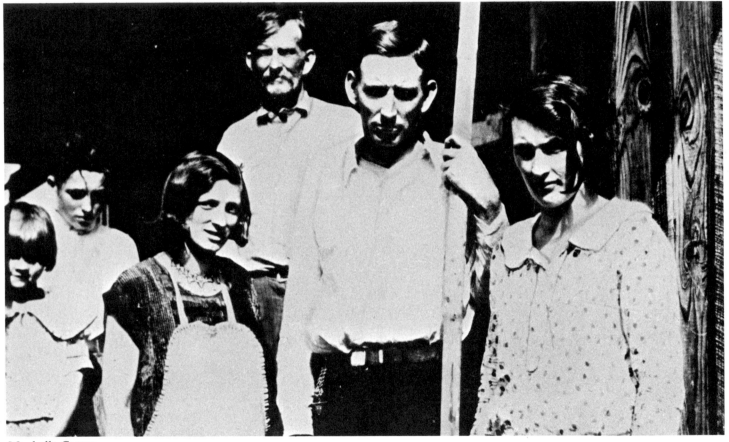

Maybelle Carter,
A. P. Carter, Sara Carter.
(Courtesy WSM)

Floyd Collins or the Scopes trial.

It is Ralph Peer who remains the most noted talent scout. He worked first for Okeh and then for Victor and then as music publisher—the company he founded is now known as Peer International. Chief among his achievements are the discoveries of Jimmie Rodgers and the Carter Family. Both took place in midsummer of 1927, and a close look at Rodgers and the Carters—the land they come from, their repertoire and manner—will tell us much about the early world of country music.

The place-names of southwestern Virginia—Bony Blue, Dungannon, Chilhowie, Castlewood, Abingdon, Scott County—tell you its settlers came from Scotland and northern

England. They tell you, too, of their history, of the Battle of Culloden (in which England's subjugation of Scotland was completed), of their religious heritage (fundamentalist Presbyterian), and of their musical heritage. To this new land they brought Scottish, Irish, and English ballads. Perhaps the soft hills and deep valleys, sudden rocky inclines, quick streams and rivers reminded them of home.

The Clinch Mountains cut through Scott County, Virginia; and on one side, in Maces Springs, A. P. Carter was born in 1891. There he died in 1960. A taciturn man, he was something of a jack of all trades: he farmed, was an expert carpenter, could shoe a horse, worked on a railroad gang, knew all there was to know about trees. And he loved music, all kinds of music, not only the ballads his mother taught him, but the fiddle tunes he heard at square dances and hoedowns, the gospel songs and hymns itinerant preachers and song teachers brought with them, blues and work songs he heard from black laborers.

His religious heritage instilled a distrust of earthly things; the tumultuous nature of his surroundings, its lush surface and tempestuous rages, spoke too of temporal impermanence. The firmer one's grip on things, the more likely they would slip away. It was best to play the guest on earth, ties loose.

While you couldn't exactly call it work, he learned you could make money by playing and singing. And though he became one of country's most important musicians, he never thought of himself as a professional. When the traveling became too exhausting and the jobs scarce, he gave up touring, radio, and making records, and spent the rest of his life as a nurseryman.

When a young man, he met a dark-haired, high-cheekboned girl in Copper Creek who played the autoharp (a lap-sized harp with an automatic chording device) and who sang in a deep, rich voice. In 1914, he married this girl, Sara Dougherty, and brought her to his Maces Springs home.

Sara had a young, blue-eyed cousin, Maybelle Addington, who played the guitar, banjo, and autoharp. Some eleven years after the marriage of A. P. and Sara, Maybelle was courted by A. P.'s brother, Ezra, who steered clear of music making. In 1926 they married. The Original Carter Family then began their career in full force: Sara sang lead and played the autoharp, Maybelle sang tenor harmony and was guitar soloist for the breaks, A. P. sang bass.

Their programs, given at church socials, in town halls, at local gatherings, were "morally fit" as an old program states —an important factor where the fiddle was apt to be thought the devil's box and the banjo heathen.

Many in the Carter clan performed, but A. P., Sara, and Maybelle were special. Their songs were familiar ones, but they played with a depth, a purity, and a modesty that brought them wide recognition.

In late July of 1927, Ralph Peer came to the town of Bristol, which straddles the Virginia-Tennessee border, on a tour to find mountain talent for Victor Records. On August 1, Peer recorded the Carter Family (three days later, he made the first recording of Jimmie Rodgers).

It is the musical style of the Carters that is their claim to importance, for they took hymns, gospel songs, blues, and ballads and made them their own. Though he wrote many songs, A. P. had no hesitation in copyrighting and claiming authorship of age-old material—there was some real justice in the act, for after A. P. touched it, it was indeed a "Carter" song. Not the least of his accomplishments is his collecting tunes the way the folk sang them.

The Carters's performances were cleansed of any extraneous "acting" in the singing, any imitation of the human voice in the playing. They trusted their music and their instruments and the drama inherent in the melodic line to carry the feeling. When you first hear the Carters you might be struck by a sense of impersonality, but the feeling has moved into the musical sounds. If the song is good, if the music true, it doesn't need extra energy of an overpowering personality.

The voice is treated like an instrument—absent are sobs and moans, crackles and laughs. The musical invention this allowed was something of a revelation: the melody played on the bass strings of the guitar, reversing the strum of the chord (part of what country musicians call "the Carter lick"), new ornaments, entrance of instruments, surprising and irregular repeats, a variety of sources for the bridge material, Maybelle raising the autoharp to her shoulder becoming one with her instrument, transference of one instrument's techniques to another (the guitar played like a banjo).

And there is the wonder of the blend of voices: the alto, Sara, carrying the melody, Maybelle providing the high harmony, and A. P. the bass harmony. This compression of a whole assortment of country playing skills and a continuance of the line of adventure they suggested is what Bill Monroe would embark on and that would result in what we know today as bluegrass—and it was what down in Texas Bob Wills would do in his Western swing bands and that would provide the base for both today's Tex-Mex sound and the California sound.

Through their records and radio appearances the Carter Family brought their music to millions in the 1930s. Families of imitators followed them—and still do.

As the years passed, the original group was expanded to include Janette, Sara and A. P.'s daughter, and Maybelle's daughters, Helen, Anita, and June Carter (now the wife of Johnny Cash and the mother of John Carter Cash), and other relatives.

Although A. P. and Sara separated in 1933, the original group continued to appear and record together all the way into the early forties. Their songs are country classics: "Wildwood Flower," "Worried Man Blues," "Keep on the Sunny Side," "Little Moses," "Jimmie Brown the Newsboy," "Wabash Cannonball," and "Little Darling Pal of Mine." (The melody of the last served Woody Guthrie for "This Land Is Your Land.") And theirs was the song that many perform as though it were the anthem of country music, "Can the Circle Be Unbroken."

Sara remarried in 1938 and later retired to California, but in the early sixties she and Maybelle made one of the best country albums, called fittingly *An Historic Reunion.* When the original group disbanded in 1942, A. P. returned to

Maces Springs but he, too, made recordings in the fifties with Sara and Janette and Joe Carter.

Mother Maybelle has never stopped performing. She is the Queen Mother of Country Music. Throughout the forties and fifties, she continued to perform and record with her daughters. The folk-music boom brought her to the attention of new audiences all over the world. As magnetic a performer as ever, she brings tears to old-timers for their memories of years and places and folks long gone; she brings tears to the young for her greatness is unmistakable.

Her son-in-law, Johnny Cash, often credits her with retrieving his life; and we respect him for so insistently recalling our debt to her and all the Carters as well.

Chet Atkins, with Maybelle Carter and her daughters June, Anita, and Helen appearing on the Grand Ole Opry. (Courtesy Les Leverett)

June Carter on Opry as Aunt Polly Carter. (Courtesy WSM)

Jimmie Rodgers was country's first big commercial star. He defined the range of country music, taking from different parts of the South all of its musical wealth, and he forged a style that proved a firm base for the future. His journey is worth remembering.

By now, the story of Jimmie Rodgers has taken on the proportions of myth. His songs and musical style determined those of all the country performers who followed him, and it often seems that even the circumstances of his life have been imitated by other performers.

June Carter.

The legend of Jimmie Rodgers starts on September 8, 1897 near Meridian, Mississippi, right near the Alabama border. Farther north, in Lafayette County, in that same year, the novelist William Faulkner was born. This is the deep South, stronghold of its deepest traditions; it is also the land of the Delta blues.

Rodgers's mother died when he was four and he was raised by his father, a section foreman for the Gulf, Mobile and Ohio railroad. Aaron Rodgers kept his son with him, no matter how far his job took him. Traveling and railroading was Jimmie's earliest education.

From the black railroad crews whom he served as waterboy, he learned to play the banjo and guitar, and he learned their songs, their blues. Rather, he absorbed them, for they became his natural expression,

> Hey, little waterboy, bring the water jug round.
> Dollar and a half a day
> My good gals waiting on Saturday night
> Just to draw my pay . . .*

It was natural, too, to become a railroad man, and he was successively a section foreman, flagman, brakeman. His banjo was always with him, and he sang on work breaks, and in the evenings in friends' parlors. It was in his nature to wander, but he married Carrie Williamson in 1920, and the next year they had their first child, Anita, and he made the attempt to settle. But his work was both a reason and an excuse to keep moving. In 1923, the news came to him in New Orleans that back in Meridian his second baby daughter had died and he had to hock his banjo to raise the fare home.

Always physically frail, he spent three months in the hospital in 1924 with tuberculosis. There could be no more exhausting train jobs. It was then that he tried in earnest to be an entertainer, and his first big job was with a medicine show (a training ground for many a country star) in which he performed in blackface.

After that, he and his family moved to Asheville, North Carolina, hoping the climate would be better for his health. A friend got him a job as a detective, for which he was particularly ill-suited, and he quit that soon and formed

* "Muleskinner Blues" (Blue Yodel No. 8), words and music by Jimmie Rodgers. Copyright 1931 by Peer International Corporation. Copyright renewed. Used by permission.

his own musical group, the Jimmie Rodgers Entertainers. For a while they had a radio show in Asheville.

Locally, the Singing Brakeman was gaining quite a reputation. He was also the Blue Yodeler. Folks knew the blues and had heard what was called the Swiss yodel but not in such a combination. Rodgers's yodel is more than a musical decoration; it is an extension of the lyric, at times a happy fireworks display, at others a lament that began when words could no longer tell the feeling.

Some of his best songs he wrote with his wife's sister, Elsie McWilliams; and with his good friend Clayton McMichen, a great and important country fiddler, he wrote "Peach Pickin Time in Georgia."

Rodgers had a way of being original with a lot of stuff he'd heard before. On his records you can hear all the country instruments: guitar and banjo of course, the fiddle, mandolin, Hawaiian string steel guitar, ukulele. And you can hear McMichen, the Carters, and Louis Armstrong, too.

The big break came in 1927 when he test recorded in Bristol for the Victor Talking Machine Company. Ralph Peer signed him for a contract, and within a year his success was sure. Within three years he was able to build a fifty-thousand-dollar mansion in Kerrville, Texas (Texas adopted him and made him an official Ranger) and own a fleet of cars.

In his last years, hospital bills and high living ate into his income, and since touring had to be restricted he depended heavily on recording. His doctors predicted he didn't have long to live, and this reality forced him to work beyond his strength to ensure his family's future.

What attracts some is the aura of tragedy about him, but though his life was sometimes sad, he is too happy a performer to be thought of as tragic. His death, though, is moving. At the age of thirty-five, after a career of only six years, he suffered a massive tubercular hemorrhage while in New York for a recording stint. Those last recording sessions, with a cot by the microphones, are the most painful moments of his legend.

The day of his death he went on an outing to Coney Island with a hired nurse. His bleeding began in the early evening, and on the night of May 26, 1933, he died in his room at the Hotel Taft.

His body was borne home, like a fallen warrior's, and every recounting of his life mentions the mournful whistle of the funeral train as it pulled into his birthplace and final resting home, Meridian, Mississippi.

His greatest legacy is his records, and through them he served as an inspiration, a living force, long after he passed away. They are not "records" from a past era, and they don't need the extra embellishments of romantic biographical trappings. The urge to glorify him is magnified by our pain over his death, and the desire to "make it up to him" for what he was robbed of by the shortness of his life.

The first astonishing quality of his recorded performances is their freshness. His talent has not aged; he doesn't sound quaint or distant. Though his first popularity came during the Depression years, and he has been made the spokesman for them, what we hear today cannot be historically defined. He transcends his period.

He was blessed with grace, both the personal grace that is bravery in face of adversity and the grace in performance whose hallmark is an easy, sure intimacy with both his material and his listeners. His performing career was limited by his illness (in "The T.B. Blues" he mocks and defies it), and he could not tour extensively. Therefore, during his lifetime, few outside the South and Southwest knew of him. Fame and adoration came posthumously, maybe not with any of the mass public recognition given to stars like Jolson, Crosby, or Sinatra, but with a deeper loyalty.

Jimmie Rodgers at nineteen.
(Courtesy Country Music Foundation Library and Media Center)

Though he has received every honor possible, his followers have made him a martyr, a suffering genius, cursed by fortune: If only he had lived longer, if only he had met the great public he deserved, if only the cloud of imminent death hadn't hovered over him. And all this is so at odds with his music, for he was an engaging, wonderful entertainer. Rodgers's case is the most dramatic of the public so identifying with *their* star that he is called upon to suffer on a gigantic scale.

Even more amazing, Rodgers is worth all the attention and tribute. Listening to his records over and over again is a double pleasure: discovery of new delights and happiness of being with a good companion. And there is something else about this guy many country artists and fans feel: he is an "example"—you want to be just like him. In fact, he *is* a hero, and he becomes one by the most surprising means.

One reason given for his stature is that he could handle so many different kinds of material: blues, hillbilly songs, cowboy, railroad, and hobo songs, sentimental and popular songs. For each category he has another voice: his ear was keyed to regional distinctions in accent and ways that born Southerners can best appreciate.

He wore many hats, you could say (and indeed he did, mostly to cover his thinning hair): brakeman's cap, straw boater, Stetson. He was the lonesome railroad man, the wandering son remembering his mom and dad, the spurned, bitter lover, the fun-loving rake. Without losing his individuality (and in performance he wore a neat suit, not any costume gear) he fit in anywhere, could be many kinds of character. He contained most of the diverse personalities of country music.

Hank Snow at his idol's grave in Meridian. (Courtesy Hank Snow)

Nothing really gets him down, for he has real pluck
and courage. In the wail and anger of "Never No Mo' Blues,"

>I'm going to be gone before long
>And then I'll hush this crazy song
>And never will sing no mo' no mo'

there is a hint of self-mockery in the extravagant description
of what he will do,

>I'll take a long ocean trip
>On a great steam ship

and of his self-pity,

>My life is a failure . . .
>I hate to say farewell
>To Mammy and my sister Nell,
>They sure will cry . . .*

that makes the pain real and also makes it temporary because
of its overstated anguish. It is the device of many of his
blues songs, like the first blue yodel, "T for Texas."

His likeable character comes through very clearly in
what sounds like his most explicit autobiographical song, "My
Rough and Rowdy Ways." Though he has settled down
with the sweetest gal, the railroad still calls him and he'll pass
a whole night drinking on the easiest provocation. Well,
he is a bounder and a rounder, rough, tough, but what can
you do about it? He just has to live with himself. In truth, there
is no meanness, no toughness in that song at all. Just a whole
lot of self-acceptance and sweet shiftlessness.

More, he sounds downright lovable, and that winsome
smile of his must have captured many a mother's heart,
probably because of the deviltry at its corners. While his
daddy's hair has turned to silver and mom is now watching
over her errant son from heaven, he really does try to be
as good as they want him to be. If he doesn't succeed, you
know he means well—and you love him all the more
for making you worry about him so.

Because he has no conceit and is not a crybaby, he
makes his sentimental songs sound true. He gives a very
balanced picture of himself—good and bad—and you trust
him to speak honestly of others.

His buoyant spirit eased the sufferings of those in the
Depression years who felt their country had failed them.
He showed them the richness of their music, and thus he
showed them their worth.

George D. Hay, "The Solemn Old Judge," Opry's mastermind, holding the steamboat
whistle he used to open the program. (Courtesy WSM)

44

3
Barn Dances
of the Air

Opryland, outside
Nashville, is a 369-acre amusement park whose theme is
American popular music: jazz, folk, standard pop, rock,
but most especially country.

The visitor wanders through a series of live musical
shows (scattered among the rides, restaurants, natural animal
habitats) including a showboat production, a Dixieland
bandstand, and a rambunctious history of country music in
which its "historic" performers are evoked through imitation.
Antique engines lead a train that winds through the park,
going from Grinder's Switch Station (in honor of Minnie
Pearl) to El Paso Station. Roy Acuff's fine collection of old
country instruments and memorabilia which is housed in
Roy Acuff's Music Hall is worth an afternoon of study.

The biggest attraction, and the guiding reason for it
all, is the new Grand Ole Opry House which seats 4,400. It is
a magnificently equipped theater that is among the best
designed and most comfortable in the country. It fulfills its

pledge that the sightlines are excellent from every one of its plush and roomy seats. The only concessions, in both meanings of the word, made to its elegant design are the popcorn and soft-drink stands on the sides of the orchestra.

This auditorium is the first specifically designed for the Opry show, and the lobby is lined with benches from the previous Opry house, Ryman Auditorium in downtown Nashville.

Behind the stage area is another world—one that provides the most complete and technically advanced television and recording equipment available.

The whole enterprise is sponsored by the National Life and Accident Insurance Company, which also owns station

The Grand Ole Opry House at Opryland.

WSM, over whose waves were first heard the fiddles of the Grand Ole Opry. Opryland is an expression of where country music as an industry is today. Some feel that it is wide-ranging and democratic; others insist that it has lost its individual character and strength in the attempt to make it pleasing to everyone.

For many, country music is Opry, and the nostalgia for the old days is bound up with past Opry stars, with the memory of listening to the Saturday-night broadcasts. In its own promotion material, Opry reinforces the idea that it virtually originated country music, and that only the greatest of country stars appeared on its broadcasts. Certainly, Opry centered the country-music industry in Nashville.

In its official biography, Opry neglects to mention that George Hay, "The Solemn Old Judge," the show's chief architect and first announcer, and the coiner of its name, worked for WLS in Chicago before joining WSM, and that Opry wasn't the first "radio barn-dance program." Hillbilly music had been on the air long before Hay's initial November 25, 1925 broadcast. One earlier starter, Chicago's "National Barn Dance" (over WLS), was more popular than Opry until the late thirties.

Just as for the early record industry, the radio stations were taken by surprise at the tumultuous response to old-time music.

George Hay's first program for WSM featured a blind

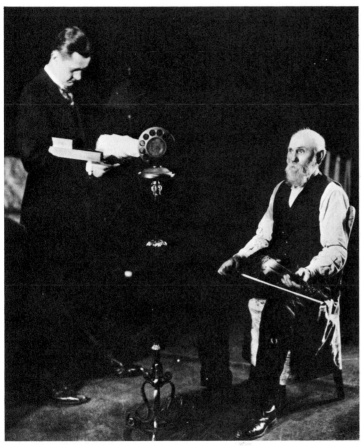

George Hay with Uncle Jimmy Thompson, Opry's first performer. (Courtesy WSM)

Harmonica player, DeFord Bailey. Opry's only Black regular, also the first entertainer to be recorded in Nashville. (Courtesy Les Leverett)

eighty-year-old fiddler, Uncle Jimmy Thompson, and his niece Eva Jones. Not much was expected of this show, but after Thompson played a few numbers, calls and telegrams with requests poured into the station. An immediate smash, the show was moved from Studio A to B to the spacious Studio C to accommodate the swarm of people who turned up to watch the program live. The crowds grew bigger, and the show was moved again to the Hillsboro Theater, then to a tabernacle in East Nashville, once more in 1939, to the War Memorial Auditorium, but that wasn't big enough either. In 1941, Opry packed up, moved again, and settled at Ryman Auditorium, an 1891 structure built by Tom Ryman for an evangelist preacher named Reverend Sam Jones. A balcony had been added in 1897 for The Confederate Veterans' reunion, and with such traditional associations there could not have been a more suitable home for Southern popular music.

This is the house that means Opry for fans, and though gutted and unused, it is a major sightseeing attraction for Nashville visitors. The feelings evoked by this great center of country music are fierce. A reporter for *The New Yorker* who was sent down to cover the opening of Opryland house wrote of his distress at the desertion of Ryman, the discarding of the place where the great performers had appeared and broadcast (though only from 1941 onward). It seemed to him such a betrayal of his youth and of the show's homespun, old-fashioned, but nevertheless glamorous,

Preparations for the last Opry show at Ryman Auditorium.

The last audience at Ryman Auditorium.

appeal that he didn't bother to make the trek to Opryland and
just stayed in his hotel room and listened to the broadcast
of the opening of the new auditorium.

Few performers, though, share such an extreme
sentimental attachment—they insist that backstage at Ryman
was hell.

George Hay's choice of a name was almost uninten-
tional. The program which preceded Opry on the air was
a classical-music hour, hosted by Dr. Walter Damrosch, a
conductor of the New York Philharmonic. The last selection
on one show was a new composition musically imitating
the rushing of a locomotive. In his introduction, Damrosch
apologized for it, because, he stated, there was no room

Backstage during the last Ryman show.

for realism in serious music.

When Hay's program came on, he announced, ". . . from here on out for the next three hours we will present nothing but realism. It will be down to earth for the earthy." Then DeFord Bailey, Opry's first and only regular black entertainer (fired some fifteen years later for supposedly having only a limited repertoire) played "Pan American Blues" on his harmonica. Hay then announced, "For the past hour we have been listening to music taken largely from Grand Opera, but from now on we will present the Grand Ole Opry."

The words were an effective nose-thumbing at Damrosch's snobbish, and inaccurate, definition, and therefore at Culture and the East. "Grand Ole Opry" stuck—both self-parody and an embrace of a stereotype. Hay's words also provided an important country-music position statement: earthy for the earthy.

For all of its history, Opry has represented for country audiences the epitome of glamour, success, wealth, and artistry—almost all of today's performers aspired to being an Opry performer in their childhood. Elsewhere in America, the dream would be to become a Hollywood star, but the difference between Hollywood and Opry is revealing. Opry stars work hard to deny that special aura that separates stars from ordinary folk, and Opry itself is more like a performing community.

The effect is that of a large, happy family, where everyone is connected and works together. The formula works, for the show is superbly produced; Hal Durham, general manager, is the man who selects the performers and arranges

Jam Up and Honey (Honey Wilds on right). Blackface comedians were a holdover from minstrel days, and were a staple of early Opry and "National Barn Dance." (Courtesy Les Leverett)

the program order—and he rules all with a firm hand. The shows are solidly booked months in advance (there is one evening show on Friday, two on Saturday, and, during the summer, matinees on both days as well).

Since its beginnings, people have traveled hundreds of miles on the off chance of getting one of the unreserved tickets. Opry is the greatest musical smash ever, and its performance record exceeds by a large margin the five longest-running Broadway hits combined—as does its attendance record.

Because of its great performers, Opry retains its importance in country music. It is a stronghold of tradition —though less musical tradition than social. At one time Opry guaranteed success, but today performers can earn much more playing tour dates without having to accommodate themselves to Opry's schedule, and a hit record or television appearances are more helpful to a career than being an Opry regular. Nevertheless, Opry membership provides a firm base for many performers, and is a method of insurance for all.

In its earliest years, it presented instrumentalists and comedians. The instrumental groups had fine hillbilly names like the Possum Hunters, the Gully Jumpers, and the Fruit Jar Drinkers. But these whimsical names were a cover for the finest musicians, like Arthur Smith and His Dixie Liners. Fruit Jar Drinkers were Kirk and Sam McGee who remained Opry stars for years. So, too, did Herman and Lewis, the Crook Brothers, whose group has often been reorganized to include members of some of the other original groups. In recent years, these mainstays have received new attention

Dr. Humphrey Bate and His Possum Hunters, the first of the WSM show's string bands. (Courtesy WSM)

for their artistry. You can spot an educated country fan by his response to the very announcement of these men's names, for rightly they are to be revered.

The top star of the early years was Uncle Dave Macon, the Dixie Dewdrop. A man of incredible vitality and a storehouse of early country music, Macon joined Opry in 1926 at the age of fifty-six. It had been only eight years before that Macon had become a professional entertainer, beginning on the Loew's theater circuit as a vaudeville entertainer. He dressed like a country gentleman, and stomped away while he played his five-string banjo. He was a brilliant raconteur and an extraordinary singer as well, as his records attest.

"The King of Country Music," Roy Acuff, joined Opry in 1937, and virtually altered the program's emphasis by shifting the "featured" performer from an instrumentalist to a vocalist.

Acuff was born in 1903 in Maynardsville, Tennessee, and was a star athlete in high school. What he wanted most to be was a baseball player, and his ability was so great that he trained with the New York Yankees in their summer camp in Florida. During baseball practice he suffered a sunstroke, and he has never fully recovered from its effects. That ended his baseball ambitions, and during his recovery he worked on his music. In the early thirties he joined a medicine show whose star was another legendary country name, Clarence Ashley (a performer rediscovered and recorded in the early sixties by Ralph Rinzler).

In a few short years, Acuff found his own voice, and his own manner —and it was of the very traditional mountain style (his group was called the Smoky Mountain Boys, and some of its members perform daily on a small bandstand in front of the Opry house in Opryland. When Roy is around, and he is most times, he will join them on the fiddle). Unashamedly sentimental, Acuff can cry during his songs, and it's his mournful, wailing manner that he is best known for, though his ability with a Yo-Yo is a trademark, and his easy, relaxed, happy manner has brought him the greatest devotion of his audience. "The Wabash Cannon Ball," a song the Carters made popular and which tells of the train that takes hoboes to heaven, and "The Great Speckled Bird," a religious song of ultimate salvation, were Acuff's earliest hits, and they remain his most requested numbers.

His career has ranged far beyond his Opry connection, and he composed and rearranged a number of songs, like "The Precious Jewel" and "Beneath that Lonely Mound of Clay." It was probably this aspect of his talent that encouraged him to join forces in 1942 with Fred Rose, an important songwriter in his own right, to form the first Nashville-based, exclusively country-music publisher, Acuff-Rose. That proved to be a major factor in making Nashville the Capital of Country Music.

Sam McGee, Arthur Smith, Kirk McGee. Three of country's greatest musicians, all with Opry from its beginnings. (Courtesy Les Leverett)

Dave Macon.

The great Delmore Brothers (right, Rabon; left, Alton) with Dave Macon. Especially noted for their adaptation of deep-South black music. Their recordings are collectors' treasures. (Courtesy Les Leverett)

The Crook Brothers Band. Top row, left to right: Herman Crook, Lewis Crook.
Bottom row, left to right: Blythe Poteet, Kirk McGee, Billy Stone. (Courtesy Les Leverett)

The Dixie Clodhoppers. Until the late thirties, Opry's main feature was string bands, and this is one of the most fondly remembered.
Left to right: Amos Binkley, Gale Binkley, Kirk McGee, Tom Andrews. (Courtesy Les Leverett)

Roy Acuff, with Lonnie "Pap" Wilson. (Courtesy WSM)

Acuff even spent some time in Hollywood, making eight feature movies, the first of which was the 1940 *Grand Ole Opry*. Others include *Night Time to Memphis, Cowboy Canteen* (Acuff, though, was never a cowboy star and in live performance always appears in sport jacket and slacks), and *Home in San Antone*.

Though his try for the governor's office proved unsuccessful, Acuff's achievement is so great and so widely acclaimed that his is probably the most glorious of country-music careers. In performance, the qualities that make him the mighty force he is are easily apparent—love for the music and devotion to his audience.

Roy Acuff.

Minnie Pearl

After Acuff came a succession of outstanding male vocalists, like the Texas-born Ernest Tubb, who first modeled his style on Jimmie Rodgers and later brought to Opry a hint of the raucous sound developed in Texas honky tonks. Eddy Arnold, the lead singer of Pee Wee King and the Golden West Cowboys, stepped out of their ranks and became "The Tennessee Plowboy," the first to successfully alter his original country style so that his popularity could have a broader national base. (Dinah Shore, too, it is often forgotten, began as a country singer.) Opry's next big vocal star spent a short time with Opry—but it was epoch making, as was his whole career, and that was Hank Williams.

A quick look at Opry's recent roster will show the variety the show strives to maintain and give a clue to its past history.

Next to Roy Acuff, Minnie Pearl has come to symbolize the spirit of the Grand Ole Opry more than anyone. Instantly recognizable in her flouncy dress and her hat with the price tag still affixed, she has offered a welcome comic interlude to the string of musical acts which dominate the Opry. Whether paired with Rod Brasfield or alone, recounting in irrepressible falsetto the exploits of Brother or Uncle Nabob in Grinder's Switch, or her own eternally unsuccessful search for a man, Minnie Pearl has delighted audiences since the late 'thirties.

In real life she is Sarah Ophelia Colley Cannon, an urbane and cultured woman of the world. Before becoming a professional comedienne at the age of twenty-eight, Minnie had

Minnie Pearl, the Duke of Paducah (Whitey Ford), Frog Milhouse (Smiley Burnette). Ford was the main "Renfro Valley Barn Dance" comic, and Burnette made a Hollywood career as Autry's sidekick. (Courtesy WSM)

Lulu Belle and Red Foley. Major stars of "National Barn Dance." Lulu Belle (Myrtle Cooper) teamed with Scotty (Scott Wiseman), and Red (Clyde) Foley began as a member of the Cumberland Ridge Runners. (Courtesy CMA)

been a school teacher, so the comic character she created has always been an amusing antithesis of the real person. Sarah Cannon, long and happily married to Henry Cannon, is active in community affairs, and is, incidentally, extremely well-heeled. She and Henry live in a beautiful, rambling house next door to the Governor's Mansion in South Nashville.

Of the old-timers, there are Bill Monroe, "The Father of Bluegrass"; and Lester Flatt. Earl Scruggs, who once performed with Flatt in Monroe's band and later as Flatt's partner, appeared on the Opry for a while after they broke up, but never in the same segments with Flatt. Del Wood, "Queen of the Ivories," is the only Opry keyboard artist, and other women performers include Loretta Lynn (a homespun girl from Kentucky who joined in 1962),

Dolly Parton, Barbara Mandrell, Skeeter Davis, and Jan Howard. Among the men are Porter Wagoner, Marty Robbins, Bill Anderson, Roy Drusky, and Hank Snow.

It is an illustrious troupe. There have been defections, most notably Tom T. Hall, and there have been those who have had great careers without the Opry imprimatur: Charlie Rich, Charley Pride, Merle Haggard, Johnny Rodriguez, Tanya Tucker, Kris Kristofferson.

Opry's faults and limitations are obvious, but like the rest of the music of which it is an aspect, Opry sneakily finds a way not only to survive but to keep pace. The changes are slow, but they happen.

Opening night at the new Opry House.

The only rival of importance to Opry's ultimate triumph was "National Barn Dance" from Chicago—and it was with this program that Opry's George Hay served his apprenticeship. In its second week of operation, during April of 1924, station WLS (the call letters standing for "World's Largest Store" because the station was owned by Sears), broadcast a program of fiddle music played by Tommy Dandurand which brought forth an enormous response from the listening audience.

To satisfy the musical tastes of the German and Scandinavian immigrants who settled in the Midwest, "National Barn Dance" provided a wide range of entertain-

Dave "Stringbean" Akeman joined Opry in 1942. A comic star, he also played banjo with Lew Childre and the Monroe Brothers. After his tragic death in 1973, a memorial tree in his honor was planted in front of the new Opry House.

Jerry Clower.

ment, though its core was mountain songs—as its first star, Bradley Kincaid (the Kentucky Mountain Boy), insisted they be called. Kincaid sang traditional ballads from the British isles, like "Barbara Allen," but in the native Kentucky style—nasal, high-pitched and uninflected—and with an emphasis on the sentimental. In the early forties, Kincaid followed Hay to Opry.

Gene Autry spent two years in the early thirties with "National Barn Dance," and the singer most closely identified with the program was Grace Wilson, who during her thirty-six years with it, endeared herself with deep-voiced renditions of popular songs.

Comedian duos were a mainstay throughout the program's history, and the list of famous names is extraordinary, among them: Homer and Jethro, Amos and Andy (then known as Correll and Gosden), and Fibber McGee and Molly.

Like the Opry, the show sent out touring companies starring the radio performers, and sometimes trying out new talent—bluegrass innovator Bill Monroe played on one of the tours though never on the program itself.

During the thirties the show featured a string band with a square-dance group called the Cumberland Ridge Runners, which had been organized by John Lair, the program's music director. A Kentucky boy, Lair had always dreamt of setting up a town in Renfro Valley devoted to maintaining a pioneer tradition and look. Finally in 1939 Lair's dream came true and a by-product was one of the best barn-dance programs, the "Renfro Valley Barn Dance." Among the fine performers associated with this Kentucky-based and strictly country program were Red Foley and Whitey Ford, the Duke of Paducah.

There were many other influential and fondly remembered shows but perhaps the most important were Wheeling, West Virginia's "WWVA Jamboree," among whose stars were Grandpa Jones (another Opry favorite), the Osborne Brothers (since 1964 Opry fixtures), and Elton Britt. Two programs served as minor-league Opry: "Louisiana Hayride" (both Presley and Hank Williams made their major debuts on this) from Shreveport and Knoxville's "Tennessee Barn Dance."

Oddly enough, television has never succeeded in establishing programs of such importance. Red Foley starred in the fifties on "Ozark Jubilee," a program which also featured Sonny James, Wanda Jackson, and Brenda Lee. The show lasted only three years. The forays of Johnny Cash, Glen Campbell, Jimmie Dean, Ernie Ford, and Roger Miller into network shows have not proved particularly beneficial for the furtherance of country—if anything, they varnished up their stars so that one couldn't see the vitality of the performers.

There are two exceptions: one is the cleverly produced annual Country Music Awards; the other is the country

Roy Clark and Chet Atkins tuning up for a "Hee Haw" performance.

61

version of "Laugh-In," a show that has proved more durable than the one it was patterned on. It is, of course, "Hee Haw," with its driving forces Buck Owens, the amazingly versatile Roy Clark, and featuring Grandpa Jones, Junior Samples, and Minnie Pearl.

Of all the country-music radio programs, the oddest and most interesting group is the Mexican border station shows on which the Carters appeared.

Because the United States had usurped the broadcast band of airwaves without including Mexico, that country got revenge by encouraging United States entrepreneurs to set up stations south of the Texas border. These stations were allowed to transmit with power wattage far in excess of what U.S. law allowed. To this day, the programs on these stations devote themselves to hard-line religion, medicinal tonics, right-wing politics, and country. Because of the initial call letter of these stations (XEG, XENT, XERA) they became known as the X-stations. The actual studio of XERA was in Del Rio, but the program was transmitted across the Rio Grande from Villa Acuna.

These programs were important because they helped not only the Carters, but also the Delmore Brothers, Mainer's Mountaineers, and the Pickard Family in reaching a wide public, and the effect has been enormous—providing a steady audience through the Southwest and the Midwest for our native music.

John Henry Faulk and Archie Campbell.

Buck Owens.

Tex Ritter. (Courtesy Country Music Foundation Library and Media Center)

4
Western Swing and Swinging Westerns

The music of Texas that added "Western" to what is "country-and-Western" was not the cowboy laments and ballads or the range songs with Spanish overtones, but it was swing, Western swing.

It was a big-band sound designed for dance halls, and its greatest epoch was contemporary with the big bands of Tommy Dorsey and Benny Goodman. For the South and Southwest, the big band was Bob Wills's, and this large ensemble caused a revolution in country whose result wasn't clear until recent years.

Western swing was a freewheeling blend of jazz, Dixieland, Hawaiian steel guitar, mariachi music, pop songs, old-timey tunes—and it brought horns to country. Today, Danny Davis and His Nashville Brass brings the shivers to those who don't like their country music diluted, but the sound has been around for a long while and is in truth an integral part of the country spectrum.

The development of Western swing was haphazard

rather than planned, but it took the unique condition of the state of Texas to allow all the disparate elements to combine.

From south of the border came the Mexican strains of an insistent rhythm and loud horns; and the new settlers from the Southern states brought their traditional music and the fiddle. New Orleans did give birth to the blues and to the Dixieland rhythms. By the late twenties a new rural style was in its initial stages of development and it blossomed brilliantly through the thirties, forties, and fifties.

Bob Wills was born in 1906 in Limestone County, Texas, and as a child he worked in the cotton fields with blacks whose blues he made his own—throughout his life he always spoke reverently of Bessie Smith. From his father he learned to play the fiddle, and by the age of ten he was able to play well enough to fill in for the elder Wills. The fiddle has always been the heart of his music, though he was at first reluctant to perform as a solo instrumentalist.

In 1929, he moved to Fort Worth, serving, like so many entertainers of those days, an apprenticeship with a medicine show, and appearing in blackface. Later, as a bandleader, his hallmarks were his cries of "Take it away, Leon" and his whoops and swoons of excitement at the playing of one member or another. Not only were these unabashed cries of delight, they were skillful "medicine show" techniques for enlivening the audience's response.

Wills teamed up with Herman Arnspiger, a guitarist, to form the Wills Fiddle Band, and a year later, in 1930, Wills added three new members, including the vocalist Milton Brown. Among their regular dance-hall engagements was one at Fort Worth's Crystal Springs, which was notorious for being the favorite haunt of Bonnie and Clyde.

The band was renamed the Light Crust Doughboys when they began a radio show in Fort Worth sponsored by the Burrus Mill and Elevator Company which made Light Crust Flour. The announcer of the program happened to be W. Lee O'Daniel, the president of Burrus Mill, and who was a song writer too, with such country standards as "Beautiful Texas" and "Put Me in Your Pocket" to his credit. In later years, O'Daniel, with campaigns loaded with country entertainment, became governor of Texas and a United States senator. O'Daniel was also to become a thorn in Bob Wills's side, for he insisted that Wills stop playing at dances and other gigs on the side. This caused Milton Brown to leave the organization and form his own band, one of the most renowned of the thirties, Milton Brown and His Musical Brownies.

Wills replaced Brown with the singer most closely associated with him, Tommy Duncan, who was able to move through all the musical styles that make up the conglomerate called Western swing.

In the summer of 1933, O'Daniel fired Wills, for reasons that have been variously explained as salary disputes, Wills's drinking, and Wills's wish to add his brother, Johnnie

Lee, to his band. Whatever the reason, Wills then moved to Waco and the group became known as the Playboys. That group included Bob's brother, Johnnie Lee, playing tenor banjo, Kermit Whalen on the steel guitar, and June Whalen playing rhythm guitar.

O'Daniel was not through with Bob Wills though, and sued him for advertising the fact that they were the former Doughboys. He didn't stop there, for he had Wills's program replaced with one of his own, and Wills had to move on again, this time to Oklahoma City, and from there to Tulsa where he finally managed to extricate himself from O'Daniel's harassment by paying for his own radio show. It was the years in Tulsa, 1934–42, that was, as Wills himself acknowledged, his greatest period.

This was the time of Wills's greatest experiments with band sounds, and he was willing to try anything, to include any instrument and any combination to achieve the very best. To the base of fiddle, steel guitar, piano, and tenor banjo were added trumpet, saxophone, clarinet, and trombone— the jazz band combined with the string band. Keeping a danceable rhythm, it became swing.

Wills's showmanship—his calling out the names of band instrumentalists for their solos, singing along, parading around throughout the number—made him distinctive, but the legacy to modern country has been aptly described by the Country Music Foundation's Executive Director Bill Ivey: "The use of drums, the employment of jazz-style solos, the use of amplified fretted instruments, the role of the steel guitar as a solo and background music: all of these elements of modern country performance style can be traced to the influence of Western Swing bands."

A great addition to the Tulsa-based Texas Playboys— as they were now called   was the steel guitarist Leon McAuliffe, who, in a brilliant act of revenge, Wills had recruited from O'Daniel's group. A country-and-Western classic is McAuliffe's "Steel Guitar Rag," a number that was his first solo with Wills, and though thoroughly restyled by McAuliffe, is a reworking of a "race" number called "Guitar Rag." With Wills, McAuliffe wrote the Playboys biggest hit, "San Antonio Rose."

In the early forties Bob Wills and His Playboys appeared in a number of those Western musicals that Hollywood churned out weekly, but the war dissolved the group as each member enlisted. After the war, Wills formed a new organization, a reduced band with less brass, but using the guitar as a replacement for the sound of horns. There was a consequent re-emphasis of the prominence of the fiddle—Wills's instrument—with the additions of Johnny Gimble and Keith Coleman to the band. A jazz improvisation on the fiddles had long been a standard Wills device.

Though the big-band era was at an end, Wills kept his popularity, and steady bookings, until the mid-fifties, but illness and bad investments took their toll. And by the mid-sixties he had to give up entirely any regular performing.

In 1968, Bob Wills was elected to the Country Music Hall of Fame, even though throughout his career he did not think of himself as a "country" artist. "Country" knew differently, for he had put his indelible stamp on the music, both in the creation of high standards of performance and in its sound.

In late 1973, the Texas Playboys—that is, the most illustrious of them: McAuliffe, Al Stricklin, Leon Rausch, Gimble, and Coleman—joined with Wills for an album of their greatest hits. Hearing of this plan, one country great remembered his childhood in Bakersfield, California, and how he would sneak into Bob Wills's appearances. Then his dream was to one day be a Texas Playboy; in 1973 he asked if he could join this reunion session. On the record, called *For the Last Time*, that Bakersfield boy, Merle Haggard, sings on three cuts and joins in the fiddling.

Wills died in 1975; through his music he enriched the country experience, and in today's performances of so many country stars you can almost hear Bob Wills saying "Take it away, Merle and Waylon and Chet. . . ."

The cowboy is the American mythic hero, and his stance, his clothes, his speech, and his music have been adopted by most country stars. It is seen not only in dude attire—custom-made for the stars by Nudies of Hollywood—but country performers often take on the character of the Western hero. For years, Johnny Cash has appeared as the Man in Black, and when he comes on stage in a long frock coat he looks like a frontier minister or a judge; when he wears a simple black Western shirt and slacks, he is the tough hombre dressed up, with the suggestion of badness lurking around him.

That is a harkening up of the past, but the cowboy ideal has a new version, and today's men of the range are truckers and linemen, riggers and construction workers. Merle Haggard singing the theme song of the television series "Movin' On" is singing a cowboy song. The range is a highway, and the heroes are passing through; the real danger is that they might settle down, and settling down is the death of the cowboy.

The cowboy song is a type we know already, for the authentic ones, like those published by John A. Lomax in 1910, are in fact the old ballads and tunes with new lyrics, and with Spanish words, a smidgen of Cajun spicing, and some minstrel tempos. But we are left with the initial effect: these are songs of men just on the edge of civilization, eking out an existence in a world they don't trust, and fighting off the efforts to hold them down.

Western is one with country; and the greater attempt that is made to distinguish the two, the clearer it becomes that in essentials they are the same. In talking about cowboys, we will be talking about another version of country.

The Maddox Brothers and Rose. (Courtesy Country Music Foundation Library and Media Center)

Bob Wills and the Texas Playboys. (Courtesy Country Music Foundation Library and Media Center)

The image of the cowboy's life is one of freedom: his home is the range and he sleeps under the stars. He has erased all traces of the past, his rootlessness is his present, and his future is like the old soldier's—he will fade away. Today, the trucker sings to the rhythm of his engine; the cowboy sang to the rhythm of the trot of his horse. The songs are the lonesome ones of being far from loved ones, of being betrayed in love, of solitary work. There is both lament for being an outcast, and joy in being unfettered. It is the tragic romance of the individual, and there is that odd recurring theme of American individuality: it is basically antisocial. The hero of the world's greatest democracy is self-reliant, morally rigid, classless, homeless, and anticommunal. In the movies, which have devoted millions of reels to the cowboy, except for his jerk of a sidekick, his horse, and his girl who he treats with the distant courtesy due a "lady," he is not merely friendless, he is downright unfriendly. By being unfriendly, he remains pure, unsullied. It is a character trait he shares with another American hero, the hardboiled detective. You might want to *be* John Wayne, or Humphrey Bogart, but it is impossible to think they could be your friend. You'll hear that don't-tread-on-me strain in many country songs, and that is America's way of being nobly tough.

The drifter and the hobo and the cowboy are modern versions of the knight errant. They have pulled themselves out of society to go on a quest; but the quest isn't religious or selfless—it is selfish in that it avoids human contact. The great movie Western *Shane* is a conscious retelling of the legends of Arthurian knights, and the evil Shane is ridding the land of is land robbers; but once that task is finished he heads off for the unreal world that is his home. That idea of drifting off into the sunset is just like the one of Dorothy leaving the world of Oz: it is saying that this world we have been watching isn't "real," it is ideal and beautiful. To ride off leaving all the bandits in jail with peace brought back to the land is the end of a dream, a happy dream.

Country music is the last outpost of this particular American dream. It has transformed the cowboy into the trucker, the "high steel" worker, the itinerant man. The cowboys are still with us, and if we list some of the Western heroes, we'll find them awfully familiar.

Histories of country music give accountings of the "Singing Western," those vehicles which starred Ken Maynard, Gene Autry, Roy Rogers, Tex Ritter, and many others. These were films churned out cheaply—and weekly—and they conformed to a clear formula. But Western movies and country-music themes are even more deeply entwined than this obvious mixing of music and myth, and it is worthwhile to take a look at typical cowboy movies and their change over the years before focusing on those musicals they are an imitation of.

No matter what claims are made for Alaska or space, our last real frontier was the West, and we hold on to the idea that this vanished reality—where nature has not been conquered, civilization has not reached, and man is free—still exists. But it was already a fictional place when Zane Grey and Owen Wister used it for their books. Their novels were, indeed, based on fact, but that fact was so dusted with romantic visions of noble gestures that it wasn't the reality that made the impact on the public. It was a world of wide-open spaces, true free enterprise, clearly defined evil, personal morality (where killing was allowable if it was just), and heroism of the little man. The good cowboy was holding the fort until the law arrived.

The first movie epic was a Western, *The Great Train Robbery* (1903); in the silent era Dustin Farnum, Tom Mix, and even Rin Tin Tin protected us all.

Most often, the hero had to be provoked to violence, for he was basically peaceable and innocent. He was often called the Kid, as he was when played by John Wayne in *Stagecoach* or James Cagney in *The Oklahoma Kid* or Gary Cooper in *The Texan* or Robert Taylor and countless others as Billy the Kid. These kids are going through the rites of manhood, and they prove their manhood by showing they are capable of violence (for a just cause, of course).

In more recent years, the same kind of story is told in movies like *Walking Tall* and *The Trial of Billy Jack,* the favorite films of staunch country fans. There have been a host of movies lamenting the loss of the wild spaces and the cowboy's place, as do *The Wild Bunch, Lonely Are the Brave* (the horse is killed when trying to cross a highway), and *The Ballad of Cable Hogue*: in all these Sam Peckinpah movies the death of the Old West is announced by the arrival of the automobile. Like so many of America's tributes to its past, this myth is an exercise in nostalgia for the "never was," and in it there lurks the suspicion that not only is it inventing history but it is inventing character—as if the actual historical past, and our personal past, are either vacuous or disgraceful. We invent our past; we invent our personality. This fakery is the energizing agent for popular art, and is unabashedly clear in country songs.

Though it is well known that Western regalia is a costume for country stars and that it has nothing to do with their background and lifestyle, it is often forgotten that there were genuine and influential cowboy singers. In the teens and twenties, Texas produced a series of singers who also held credentials as cowpokes: from Amarillo was Eck Robertson; from Alvin, Carl Sprague; from Jefferson, Vernon Dalhart; from Waxahachie, Jules Verne Allen; from Sherman, Goebel Reeves, the Texas Drifter.

The cowboy was a drifter, and the drifter was also a hobo. The songs of these cowboy singers included the wandering tales. These laments of men without roots hit a responsive chord all over the country, and Goebel Reeves, along with Harry McClintock (who is credited with "Hallelujah, I'm A

Bum," "The Bum Song," and the most familiar version of "Big Rock Candy Mountain") were associated with the Industrial Workers of the World (IWW) movement. This connection between traditional music and the labor movement was to be later evidenced by Woody Guthrie, Pete Seeger, Will Geer (Grandpa on the television series "The Waltons"), and Aunt Molly Jackson. It is always amazing to discover America has been singing the same song in so many different ways.

Jimmie Rodgers fixed the cowboy image forever; he popularized the tradition, and it is to him that the singing cowboys we know from the movies owe a debt rather than to the tradition he borrowed from.

It was not long after the first talkie that the Western

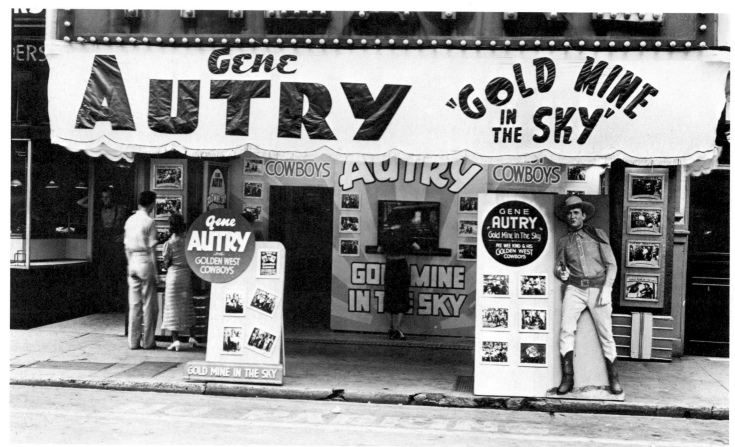

Fifth Avenue Theater in Nashville.

story and music were combined in moving pictures. The first notable example was *Sons of the Saddle*, made in 1930 and starring Ken Maynard, but it was Gene Autry who became the first major star of singing Westerns.

Born in Texas, Autry began his singing career in Tulsa, Oklahoma. He was soon contracted by Art Satherley to record for the American Record Company, and in 1930 Autry was signed for Chicago's "National Barn Dance." He styled himself after Jimmie Rodgers and the songs he sang in those early years were intentional imitations of the master.

Republic Studios brought him to Hollywood, and first put him in a Maynard feature as a singing cowhand. After doing a serial, *The Phantom Empire*, Autry was paired with a sidekick, Smiley Burnette, and soon had his horse, Champion. In films like *Mexicali Rose, Tumbling Tumbleweeds,* and *The Last Round-Up* he sang around the bunkhouse, distracted the villains with a song, sent secret messages to sheriffs in tunes.

Autry's films were not set in the Old West, nor were those of his followers, Tex Ritter and Roy Rogers, but took place in the present, or something roughly equivalent. Cowboys wore ten-gallon hats, and there was a ramshackle town and people went around on horses and the ranches were small, but there were cars and radios and records and modern conveniences. This timelessness was probably dictated by the economics of making Westerns: little money and almost no

time was spent on them.

The songs were composed especially for the features and used the familiar elements of cowboy lore. Autry wrote many of his own songs, and with Ray Whitley, composed the best-known cowboy number which is also a country classic, "Back in the Saddle Again." The words sum up almost all the cowboy-myth clichés: he's carrying his old forty-four, sleeping out every night "where the only law is right," and the song is complete with cattle calls. In 1941, he wrote with Fred Rose, later of Acuff-Rose, another country classic, "Tears on My Pillow."

Like many a Western hero, Autry appeared deceptive. He seemed slow, was pleasant looking rather than handsome,

Gene Autry comes to Nashville for the opening of his movie *Gold Mine in the Sky.* Top, left to right: J. L. Frank (known as the Flo Ziegfeld of country), Milton Estes, Sari, Autry, Sally, Jack Scaggs, Pee Wee King, Asher Sizemore. Bottom row, left to right: Abner Sims, Buddy Sizemore, Daisy Rhodes, Little Jimmy Sizemore, Curley Rhodes. (Courtesy Les Leverett)

had an easygoing manner, but when things got rough, he was tough and smart and had his wits about him. He didn't have to brandish his superiority—he just held it in reserve.

He was true country, and in 1969, this was officially recognized when Autry was elected to the Country Music Hall of Fame.

Singing Westerns were the specialty of Republic Studios, but they weren't only associated with that studio. All studios made them, and Monogram and Columbia produced just as many as Republic.

When Autry left Republic for Columbia, his slot was filled with a young man named Leonard Slye, a member of the Western singing group the Sons of the Pioneers, who first changed his name to Dick Weston, and finally to Roy Rogers. Rogers gave the Western a trifle more romance, by way of a girlfriend named Dale Evans, and an extra jauntiness with his horse Trigger.

The Sons of the Pioneers should not be passed over, for they began as a genuine Western singing group, and were movie stars in their own right. Though most of their songs were newly composed, they managed to project an air of authenticity of the range that other groups lacked. The grand master of the Western movie, director John Ford, used them prominently in two of his films, *Wagon Master* (in which they sang "Wagons West" and "Rolling Shadows in the Dust" on the soundtrack) and *Rio Grande* in which they appeared

Roy Rogers. (Photo Gordon D. Gillingham)

before the cameras.

Another great Western-movie classic utilized the talents of a singing Western star. It was Tex Ritter who sang the title song over the credits of *High Noon*. In the country-music industry no Western singer is more beloved than Ritter. First of all, Ritter was a great gentleman, and his gentle, shy manner never hid the fact that he was a man of great culture. Of the many who credit Ritter with giving them a helping hand at a turning point in their careers, I will list only a few: the late Jim Reeves, Hank Thompson, Jan Howard, Buck Owens, Charlie Walker.

Ritter was born in Murvaul, Texas, and attended the University of Texas where he studied law. Competing with his ambition to be a lawyer was his love for the history and music of the West, and as a young man he could name among his friends the musicologist John A. Lomax, Western historian J. Frank Dobie, and folksinger Huddie Ledbetter.

Deciding to follow his heart, Ritter made his way to New York to try for a singing career. He got a singing role in the play *Green Grow the Lilacs* by Lyn Riggs (later to be transformed into *Oklahoma!*) and understudied the lead, Franchot Tone. The next two plays he appeared in were not successful, but by this time Ritter was forging a solid radio career, in radio's first Western serial, "The Lone Star Ranger," and a popular children's program, "Cowboy Tom's Round-up." There was also "Tex Ritter's Campfire," and he was featured

Porter Wagoner and Tex Ritter, 1973. (Photo Les Leverett)

singer for New York's "WHN Barn Dance" (that station is now New York City's country-music station).

Since Autry had established the commercial success of the singing Western, the search was on for others, and Ritter seemed a natural. Besides, his credentials for the role were better than those of the rest. His first film was *Song of the Gringo* and it was in this that he introduced one of his hits, "Rye Whiskey." With his own wonder horse, White Flash, Ritter starred in over seventy films for Columbia, Monogram, and Republic, among them *Ridin' the Cherokee Trail, Trouble in Texas* (with Rita Cansino, later named Hayworth), and a host of other efforts that were undistinguished and indistinguishable from one another, but that created for those who

Judy Lynn. (Courtesy Judy Lynn)

grew up on them an ideal way of being gallant, brave, tough, and gracious, all at the same time.

The songs most identified with him include such standards as "Hills of Wyoming," "New Moon Over My Shoulder," "Life Gits Teejus, Don't It," "Have I Stayed Away Too Long," and "Boll Weevil." His biggest hits were "Jingle, Jangle, Jingle" and "Hillbilly Heaven."

In the mid-sixties, Ritter moved to Nashville and became something of an elder statesman. He appeared with the Grand Ole Opry, and made unsuccessful bids for governor and the United States Senate. He did, though, become president of the Country Music Association, and in 1964 was the second living person to be elected to the Country Music Hall of Fame.

While Ritter, Autry, and Rogers were the biggest of the singing Western stars, there were other, fondly remembered followers, like Dick Foran, Rex Allen, Jimmy Wakely (who often recorded with Margaret Whiting), and Eddie Dean.

The Western influence extended beyond the men to the tradition of the companion cowgirl. The most famous of the legendary figures were the outlaw Belle Starr (immortalized on film by Gene Tierney), sharpshooter Annie Oakley (at different times portrayed by Barbara Stanwyck, Ethel Merman, and Betty Hutton), and Bill Hickok's pony-express-rider, scout-for-Custer girlfriend Calamity Jane (in the thirties played by Jean Arthur and in the early fifties by Doris Day). All of these displayed the desperate but only way of competing in a man's world: they dressed and behaved like men. Today, singers like Judy Lynn and Lynn Anderson, true and accomplished riders and rodeo performers, perform in cowgirl getups, but the outfit is no statement of competition: it is sexy.

The queen of the movie cowgirls was Roy Rogers's girlfriend, Dale Evans. They married in 1947, after the death of Roy's first wife, and Dale Evans began her career as a pop singer; Hollywood cast her as a cowgirl.

A more important cowgirl was Patsy Montana (though she was born in Arkansas) who starred as part of the Prairie Ramblers on the WLS "National Barn Dance." The Ramblers brought to the North the musical innovations of Western swing, and Patsy, who wore cowgirl's skirt and blouse, was noted for her yodel. She is a crucial figure in upgrading the place of women in country, and her greatest hit was, naturally, "I Want to Be a Cowboy's Sweetheart," which sold a million copies in 1936.

It was the West that conquered country music, most visibly in dress and manners. But these were appurtenances. There was a new style that was being forged—the Jimmie Rodgers manner was imitated by those who entertained in raucous barrooms. It was the beginning of the "honky-tonk" style.

Hank Williams and friend. (Courtesy CMA)

5
Honky
Tonkin'

Ernest Tubb estimated that seventy-five percent of current country musicians are Texas born and bred. Whatever the actual figure, Nashville's country performers have Texas in their blood and in their style and in their twang.

Texas gave the cowboy look to country, but what counts for more is a vocal and instrumental style that overhauled the familiar musical signatures of plaintive wails and lonely cries. That style has the catch-all name "honky tonk"; it was born in the thirties in Texas dance halls, bars, and saloons.

East Texas, first populated by Southerners who brought with them their cotton-plantation culture (decaying mansions still spot the area), was the site of the state's oil boom in the 1920s. Rigs overran the pine-covered hills, swamps, and scrublands, and the new industry caused farmers to settle in boom towns, but didn't rid these riggers of their rural ways. What with Prohibition, and after that local dry laws, taverns were kept outside town limits, often near truck farms. If liquor couldn't be served outright, many clubs provided set-ups, and one could slip into a glass of soda water something stronger that was wrapped in brown paper.

Oil workers, laborers, truckers, and farmers hell-raised and danced to the old-timey music—but the local fiddlers and singers and pickers had to make a lot of noise to be heard and to hold the attention of the crowd. There had to be a pounding beat and clear, loud singing and lyrics that were ruggedly realistic.

A singer had to scream his whine about love's troubles, the hell of work. He'd be furious and wild rather than angry, and he'd be raunchier, rowdier, funnier, more showman than ever.

Honky tonk put an edge on the lifestyles of country musicians: drinkin', singin', late hours, crazy behavior, wearin' yourself out.

What a training ground honky tonks proved to be (and still are)!

Among the East Texas honky tonks are the Reo Palm Isle Ballroom, Danceland, the Roundup Club, and the Horse-shoe Lounge. "Saturday night," observed Paul Hemphill in *Country Music* magazine, "is the big one. Country music for the all-white, over-thirty set. Admission is $1.50 and you get your hand stamped at the door. Red-sequined dresses and Levis and gold slippers. 'When they belly up and start to do the Cowboy Shuffle with those big old heavy belt buckles,' Ernest Tubb's drummer once told me, 'it'll make the sparks fly.' " Sunday night a black band is brought in—and the place is packed tighter than ever.

Ernest Tubb was born south of Dallas in Ellis County, and what he wanted to be when he grew up was a cowboy movie star. He defined that ambition when he heard Jimmie Rodgers sing, then he wanted to sing just like Rodgers did. He spent his early years imitating Rodgers, and he managed to meet Rodgers's widow who gave him advice and aid, with the caution that he'd be better off trying to sound like himself rather than her late husband.

He began to carve out a career for himself on local Texas radio shows, and at honky tonks where he developed his distinctive phrasing—full of unexpected pauses and sud-den slurs and slides that hold the listener's attention. He achieved enough fame to be summoned to Hollywood to try to be yet another singing Western star. But in spite of a lead in *Fighting Buckaroo* he didn't catch on. Back to Texas he went, and there he found a job as a goodwill ambassador for a flour company. He entertained housewives who were out shopping by getting on top of the company car and singing them cowboy songs. More important, he began to write songs that showed off his special gifts. One was "I'll Get Along Somehow" and another, the song that made him an overnight star, was "I'm Walking the Floor Over You."

That was the hit that brought him to the stage of the Grand Ole Opry, and in January, 1943, Tubb became a regular. With his band, the Texas Troubadours, he averages over 250 nights annually on the road. But he has always made it back to the Opry for Saturday nights, and he opened his own music store opposite the Ryman Auditorium. After the Saturday-night Opry performance, Tubb broadcasts his own show, "Midnight Jamboree," where he gathers other stars and showcases new talent. Since its inception the show has featured Jimmie Rodgers recordings on every broadcast.

Over the years Tubb has had a steady string of hits, including "Rainbow at Midnight," "Soldier's Last Letter," "Missing in Action," "Too Old to Cut the Mustard," and his

Ernest Tubb.

At Ernest Tubb's Midnight Jamboree.

81

Ernest Tubb and Hank Snow, with a Jimmie Rodgers record plaque. (Courtesy Hank Snow)

Hank Snow.

Hank Snow. (Courtesy Hank Snow)

Hank Snow.

Hank Snow.

83

famous duet with Red Foley, "Goodnight, Irene." In 1965 he was elected to the Country Music Hall of Fame, and his son Justin is a member of Opry and a notable country writer and performer.

Tubb is the man who brought the honky-tonk sound to Opry, and that sound was *the* major one in country music during the forties, best exemplified in songs like "Pistol Packin' Mama," "Driving Nails in My Coffin," and "Heading Down the Wrong Highway."

There were other disciples of Jimmie Rodgers who kept closer to his sound, and most famous among them are two Canadians, Hank Snow and "Montana Slim" Wilf Carter, and Jimmie Davis, celebrated as performer of "You Are My Sunshine" and sometime governor of Louisiana.

For Tubb, the key Rodgers song was "T for Texas," and for Hank Snow it was "Moonlight and Skies." Born in Nova Scotia, Snow began his career by calling himself the Yodeling Ranger. Though his recordings date back to as early as 1936, it wasn't until 1950 that real success came to him and that he moved to Nashville to be an Opry star. With hits like "I'm Moving On," "I Don't Hurt Anymore," and "Rhumba Boogie" Snow has become one of country's immortals.

Snow has a steeliness forged in a rough early life. At twelve he was a cabin boy, and when he returned home, his stepfather threw him out and he got a job in a fish factory and went on to be a stable boy. His career was one of endless

Pee Wee King. (Courtesy Les Leverett)

touring, singing in dives and in circuit vaudeville theaters, hopes dashed just when success seemed right at hand.

When you see Snow on the stage at the Opry, bright as a Christmas tree in his embroidery and sequins, you are looking at a real pro. You can see it in his eyes. They are not star-struck or full of a stagy emotion, but are looking right back at you, calmly and clearly. Merle Haggard does the same thing. Both command your absolute attention before you know what's happening, and they do it quietly, without jumping around and screaming.

Cowboy Copas was born in Muskogee, Oklahoma, and went to Opry as a sideman for Pee Wee King. In the forties he had a long string of hits, including "Honky-Tonkin'," "Filipino Baby," "Texas Red," "Tennessee Waltz," and "Kentucky Waltz." There was an almost ten-year lull in his career, during which he played only minor dates, but in 1960 he hit paydirt again with "Alabam" and then came another success with "Signed, Sealed, and Delivered." This brought him back to Opry and his career was really moving for the second time. On March 5, 1963, he was killed in a plane crash that took the lives of two other country stars, Hawkshaw Hawkins and Patsy Cline.

Honky-tonk style, rough childhood, astonishing success, breakdown, and tragedy: all these are part of elements in the life and career of Hank Williams. His story is very different from those we have heard before, though the tale of his life contains some of the elements that are common to the lives of so many country performers. His career signals the beginning of a new era in country music and the conclusion of another.

There are traditionalists who believe the thirties was country's Golden Era. Certainly, the musical wizardry of Jimmie Rodgers, the Carters, Bill Monroe (whose long career has been almost untouched by changing musical fashions), the dazzling instrumental groups like Gid Tanner's and J. E. Mainer's—and the unvarnished sincerity of Roy Acuff, Red Foley, and Ernest Tubb have been unmatched. They were originals; their music had the vigor of "folk" music; their basic audience was limited to the South and Southwest.

This relative isolation, which had proven a fertile ground for the development of country, came to an end with World War II.

In the army, as in factories, the learning of musical favorites was a two-way street. Southerners learned Sinatra, Northerners learned Roy Acuff.

By the late forties, the forays of country entertainers into the hallowed halls of pop were increasing. For many country stars, the ideal of the Grand Ole Opry was no longer enough. The twang, nasality, heavy accent, all that high-pitched fiddlin' and corny humor made youngsters squeamish. The hick image had outworn its use. In those days, there were no throes of nostalgia for the sounds of yesteryear, for it was

a new country once again, more concerned with what we all
had in common rather than in what made us different. The
postwar boom years were smart and smug and for many,
success was no longer a myth.

Hank Williams was the first country star to command
a mass appeal throughout the land, and Nashville had been
revving up for a nationwide conquest with a skill that was
more surprising for it had little precedent.

A major record company conspired to put Williams
over on the great American public before it knew it was listening to a "hillbilly." And Williams was followed in short
order by Elvis Presley, the young Conway Twitty, Roy
Orbison, Jerry Lee Lewis. From Presley on, the emphasis on
the young and the new forced the older artists into the
shade and they deeply resented the neglect of their music
and the despoiling of traditional ways.

Williams, though, was a true country singer—by birth-
right and musical apprenticeship, and he did not so much
betray the tradition as soften it a bit. Besides, he had two
styles—deep country, which he reserved for personal appearances, and the less idiosyncratic style he used in recording.

His career is one of the most dramatic in country, and
eventually, tragedy became the reason for his celebrity and
his continuing mystique. But the bathos now surrounding his
figure is so thick that you have to search hard to find out what
his early audiences loved about him. In fact the best way to
get at him is to pay attention to the good singer and composer
he was and ignore the welter of myth. But his personal story
is that of country music's as well and, finally, cannot be
ignored.

Hank Williams was born on September 17, 1923 in
Mt. Olive, Alabama, not far from Georgiana, around and in
which most of his childhood was spent. His father, Lon, was
a sometime locomotive engineer, sometime farmer who had
suffered shell shock in World War I and its effect presumably
grew more serious over the years. In 1930 he was hospitalized.
Not until 1940 was he finally released, and those ten years
had made the break with his wife Lilly irreparable.

From childhood, Hank and his sister, Irene, a year
older than he, were involved with earning the family's income
with odd jobs like newspaper routes, shining shoes, selling
roasted peanuts. A thin, spindly legged boy, Hank was not
much good at sports but liked the self-importance his jobs
gave him—they made him street-wise and independent.

After Lon's hospitalization the financial burden became Lilly's and she proved flexible and inventive, with few
qualms about moving to a big city like Montgomery and
setting up a rooming house.

The absence of his father, with its hint of disgrace and
a bitterness on his mother's part, the domination of a strong-
willed mother and older sister were not very encouraging
grounds for Hank's boyhood. He became reticent and unsure

of himself with strangers but he was resourceful enough to discover the best mode for self-expression, music. And he was smart enough to seize opportunities wherever they were available.

He was born with a fine musical ear and he could sing with a firm, direct, expressive voice. His first serious guitar and singing lessons came from a black street entertainer, Tee-tot, who was paid with meals when there was nothing else to give him. He encouraged in the boy a feel for the blues, for the way to express heartache—little catches, the slight choking on a note that is sometimes called a sob or a tear, then whining into a phrase, slurring the words so they come closer to musical sounds, maintaining a regular, insistent beat.

At twelve, Hank made his stage debut in an amateur contest in Montgomery, singing a song of his own composition, "The WPA Blues," an apt title for those hard times. By fifteen, he was working fairly steadily with a back-up group he named the Drifting Cowboys. Lilly came with him to dates, disbursing salaries, collecting fees, and between dates the cowboys stayed in her Montgomery rooming house. Their jobs were in Alabama taverns and dance halls where your sound had to cut through the noise and audiences were quick to tell you what they thought. Moonshine, white lightning, and beer were smuggled in in Coke bottles since the areas they played were legally dry, and a frequent end to a night would be a brawl. Williams's best weapon was his guitar.

In the bigness of television, records, radio, concerts, it

Red Foley and Hank Williams. (Courtesy CMA)

Hank Williams, with Chet Atkins and Ernie Newton.
(Courtesy Les Leverett)

is often overlooked that much of country's audience like to hear "live country music" in just such taverns and roadside joints. That small-time circuit is unbeatable for getting the real action of country. Mournful really gets to you, the fastness makes you howl, the lyrics say it exactly. It is the place and sound for hell-raising and boozy companionship.

Physically unfit for military service because of a back injury from a fall (the pain was eased with drugs), Williams continued working at his music through the war. At one point he gave up and took a job in a shipping yard in Mobile, but as soon as something came up, he regathered his Drifting Cowboys.

In Baines, Alabama, while working a medicine show, he met a stunning nineteen-year-old blonde, Audrey Sheppard, who was separated from her husband and had a daughter, Lycrecia. Though his periodic drunks annoyed her, Audrey fell in love with this long, slightly stooped rake of a man whose mournful expression would suddenly break up with the widest smile. Also, she had some talent of her own and could give his group a little female sex appeal. A year later, about a month after her divorce came through, in December, 1944, she became Mrs. Audrey Williams. Audrey both honed his songs and provided an inspiration for them.

From Lilly, she inherited the responsibility of controlling Williams—a control he both needed and balked at. One can assume she inherited also the mixed feelings Hank had to those who were strong willed. Distrustful and suspicious, he was uncomfortable with guidance and concern, especially from women. Though his behavior showed every need for it, advice was the one thing he could not stomach. That ambivalence confused all who knew him.

The turning point in his career came in 1946 when he traveled to Nashville to audition his songs for Fred Rose of Acuff-Rose. To his great credit, Rose immediately saw Williams's potential both as a songwriter and performer, and he wanted to prove that he could turn Williams from a relatively unknown country singer into a national figure. With persistence, expertise, and acumen, he attacked the problem. His son, Wesley Rose, took an active part in the venture. It wasn't long before Williams had an MGM record contract and his songs were being recorded by pop stars like Tony Bennett.

The big break came with "Lovesick Blues," a song Williams didn't write. It catapulted him to the big time, and became something of a trademark.

Because of his erratic behavior, the Grand Ole Opry resisted booking him, and he served a trial period on the next-best program, Shreveport's "Louisiana Hayride" on KWKH. Williams knew what was at stake and made every effort to keep himself together.

Randall Hank Williams, or as his dad called him, "Little Bocephus," was born in Shreveport on May 26, 1949.

The next month, Hank Williams was given his chance at the Grand Ole Opry, and after the first strains of "Lovesick Blues," the usually well-behaved Opry audience went wild. Against tradition, encore followed encore, and it became Red Foley's job to quiet the audience down.

The great triumph had arrived, and earnings from his songs, records, and appearances sharply zoomed. There was money for all the cars he ever wanted and for a Nashville mansion which is today a tourist shrine. Audrey had firm ideas of what to do with the money, while Hank had almost none except to add to his gun collection. They argued over money, and an added irritant was Audrey's feeling that she no longer directed her husband's career. Fred Rose reworked many of Williams's songs and increasingly guided most aspects of his career. A woman of strong character and sharp mind, Audrey was not one to be content as the happy housewife.

Hank Williams, Jr. and Audrey Williams. (Photo Roger Schutt)

With his success came a lessening of Williams's grip upon himself. Though he made it for the all-important Saturday-night Opry appearances, at other dates he often showed up blind drunk—if he showed up at all. The more complicated the business of Hank Williams became, the more confused the man. He wanted life simple and he wanted out, yet he felt the need to sustain his career. Relief from the confusion came in an alcoholic haze. His anguish was right out in public and his audiences became fascinated with the spectacle. Often they seemed as contented with heckling and sneering as applauding him.

There were drying-out spells in hospitals followed by performances where he stumbled out, shouted back at the audience for their laughter, had memory lapses on songs he had sung hundreds of times. Indeed, he was finding his way out.

By January of 1952, Audrey filed for separation and Hank moved out of their grand house. He took rooms next to a young singer he had taken on as a protégé, Ray Price. The burden of putting up with Williams's drunks and abuse became too much for Price and he left. Five months later, Audrey received her final divorce decree. For much of the remaining days of his life, Williams would alternately plead for her to return to him and create situations that would make her furious.

On August 11, 1952, he got his walking papers from Opry. He had become impossible. If there was ever a cautionary tale of the high tolls of success, this was it. He talked of his firing as if it was a suspension, that once he pulled himself together he'd be back. "Louisiana Hayride" was happy to reenter his name on the roster.

During his last months at Opry, he had met Billie Jean Jones Eshlimar, a young girl who was going with Faron Young. Billie Jean was separated from her husband, and with Audrey gone, he concentrated his hopes on her. In the early fall of 1952 he proposed to her, and as soon as Billie

1947 Opry tour of Germany. Left to right: unidentified, Hank Williams, Audrey Williams, Rod Brasfield, Ernest Tubb, Minnie Pearl. (Courtesy WSM)

The marriage of Hank Williams and Billie Jean Jones Eshlimar. (Courtesy CMA)

Hank Williams, Jr. and Audrey Williams. (Photo Roger Schutt)

90

Jean thought her divorce final, they married, once in private and then again twice before a paying public in New Orleans. The resultant publicity was intended to bolster his fading career but it was a hopeless attempt for Williams was already a burnt-out case.

Considered poison by theater managers, Williams thought himself lucky to get a New Year's night engagement in Canton, Ohio. He would have to be driven there from Montgomery. In the course of the drive, Williams asked the driver to look for a doctor so that he could get something to ease the pain in his back. After finding one, Williams stretched out on the back seat. Some hours later, the driver became worried for Williams hadn't stirred. He stopped the car in Oak Hill, West Virginia, and touched Williams's hand. It was cold. At some time during those silent hours, Hank Williams had died. It was January 1, 1953.

His funeral in Montgomery was a mass display of grief. Followed by thousands, his body was carried first from Lilly's boarding house to the Municipal Auditorium, where Roy Acuff, Little Jimmy Dickens, Ernest Tubb, and others sang "I Saw the Light," and then to the grave. That year his records sold more than they had in any previous one. They have continually been repackaged under titles like The Immortal, The Best of, The Very Best, More Greatest Hits, The Spirit of, The Unforgettable, The Essential. A heavy string section was added to his renditions, and then there appeared full orchestral arrangements without the singer. Later, through the miracle of overdubbing, Hank, Jr. was able to sing along with his father, and he also narrated the story of Williams's life which was interspersed with his old recordings. Unpublished tapes appeared. Hollywood, with the cooperation of Audrey Williams, filmed his life story (or rather something like it), *Your Cheatin' Heart*, with George Hamilton in the lead. The dubbed-in singing voice belonged to fifteen-year-old Hank, Jr.

The question of who owned Hank Williams was a major one even while he was alive, and it became a monstrous issue after his death. The estate became a tangle and tug-of-war between Audrey, Billie Jean, Acuff-Rose, MGM, Lilly and, after Lilly's death, Irene. And there was a child who claimed Hank as father. Shortly after Hank's death, Billie Jean took to the road and appeared as *the* Mrs. Hank Williams in clubs and theaters, a role Audrey believed was more her due. An arrangement was made and Audrey embarked on a similar act, with her group, the Singing Cowgirls. Billie Jean was married again, to a fine young singer, Johnny Horton, whose life was tragically cut short in an automobile accident in Texas in 1960. Audrey Williams died in 1975.

One of the most important of today's stars, Hank Williams, Jr. is very much his own man and makes his own kind of music.

In all the writing of him there is such lavish overpraise ("the Hillbilly Shakespeare," "a genius whose like we will never see again," "America's greatest folk poet") that to talk reasonably of him is considered slander. Simply, as a musician he was not the equal of any of the greats who came before. When success arrived, there were those who suddenly noted the influences of Acuff and Tubb in his singing. It's true that those influences were there, but Williams shared that with hundreds of singers. To sing country you had to sing a bit like them. In his later interviews he himself picks up the promotion line, and there is something annoyingly (but unintentionally) coy in his tributes to Tee-tot, the old black who taught him as a youngster. He is insisting on his country credentials, true as they are, but what is always a fascinating experience in American musical history—the symbiotic relationship of black and white music—sounds here like parody.

Whatever Tee-tot's talents were, they did not spur independent genius as Arnold Schultz did for Bill Monroe or the blues did for Rodgers. What was good about Hank Williams does not need all this hype. He himself was his own kind of good.

Williams was turned into a fine money-making machine, a machine that functioned even more smoothly once he himself was out of the way. The last two years of his life were agony, not only the result of a hard childhood and strained marriage, but because in the push to success he lost himself. If from childhood he suffered from lack of confidence, those forces which demanded success robbed him of any identity whatsoever. In country circles, there is much bitter gossip about his two widows, his late mother, his sister, his publishers—and not any noticeable resentment against what finally did him in: the industry and business of making it big and staying on top. In the drive for that, there is no allowance or place for human frailty. As it is said, you gotta be tough. When his old friends tell us that Williams was his own worst enemy, they probably mean that he wasn't tough and that he had a full measure of human frailty. Seemingly, he accepted the conditions of making a big career, but his drinking was real rebellion. His fury was the most punishing kind. He didn't know where to direct it; after all, everyone wanted the "right things" for him. There was only one conclusion for him to make: there was something wrong with him.

Williams was unsophisticated, a terrible handicap for someone thrust into the limelight. It was impossible for him to cope with a world nothing had prepared him for. After he bought himself a big house, some flashy cars, elaborate clothes, what was he supposed to do with all the rest of that money?

The loneliness he sang about was of a new kind; it was born of hopelessness and despair. Unlike that of the past, it was not a familiar condition of existence to be borne bravely, one comforted by religious faith, one shared with others. In Williams's songs there are no tributes to mom and dad, no romance of the open road, no happy acceptance of shift- lessness. The religious songs, like "I Saw the Light," are revelations without mystery and they sound derivative. "Luke the Drifter," the character he assumed for his monologues, is a grandstand play of empty moralistic pieties. These monologues are not homespun philosophy; they are expressions of pain disguised, even from himself, in the verbiage of maudlin sentiment. There was an audience for Luke, so his publishers encouraged him, even to the point of writing some of the recitations for him. Happily, Luke has been forgotten.

His songs have the characteristic features of country: the accent, a steady beat, a relaxed rhythm, the imagery built on the facts of life, but the underpinning of assumed values are different. In the lonesome blues, the unhappiness is inconsolable—there is no inherent way out as in the songs of Jimmy Rodgers. Compare the desolation of Williams's "Ramblin' Man" with the contented unregenerate of Rodgers's "My Rough and Rowdy Ways." In a way unlike that of the old songs, with their expressions of mad, tight control or of threatened shootings and fury, Williams passively accepts the misery of his fortune. Because of this, his songs are often outright chilling.

The high-spirited songs also tell a different tale. "Jambalaya" and its crawfish pie and filé gumbo is fake Cajun no one Louisiana-bred could mistake, but more important it is fun and very silly. It eases the strain of having to be authentic, and plays with tradition by parodying its manner and language. Even better is the wild "Howlin' at the Moon" in which the love-crazed boy chases rabbits, spits out his teeth, pulls his hair, howls at the moon—all for love. It is the kind of antic song Roger Miller would pick up on. And "Hey Good Lookin' " is a wonderful turn of modern idiom into song. It is all new and has the swagger of Saturday night come to town and the sass of stuck-up girls.

When Williams takes us honky tonkin' we get all the shrill, raucous, flat-out, low-down great time. He had a new world to sing about, and it is not nearly so special and insular as it once was. The whole world gets the joke of it immediately—all without losing a whit of his country way.

The legend of Hank Williams grows each year, but his records are the steadying light in which we can find him. Shoo away the bloodsuckers, cut through the gauze, tear down the purple drapes. Onto a raised platform at the back of a honky tonk or onto a wide stage of a packed auditorium comes a bone-thin fellow dressed in cowboy costume embroidered with musical notes. A little nervous at first, he adjusts the microphone so that he can sing down into it. Hunched over, he'll wind his way around a blues so that your eyes will smart. Later, he'll sing a song so funny you'll hoot.

Out of the hollows of his face come those piercing eyes that go right to your heartbreak and your joy.

He wanted to be close and his greatness is that he could be when he sang, just as close as anyone had ever been to you.

In the fifties rock-and-roll seemed to be sweeping away all other forms of popular music. Youngsters turned away from traditional heroes and Opry to grind away to a faster beat. It had been supposed there could be nothing noisier than honky tonk, nothing more explicitly sexual, but rock was, and it offered a generation a sense that a musical world had been created just for them, one that was simply inaccessible to anyone over twenty.

Rock-and-roll would hold sway for over a decade, but during that time there were those who kept the faith, and held to the belief that in time they would recover the attention of the populace.

Jim Reeves.
(Courtesy WSM)

The tradition that had moved from Rodgers to Tubb to Williams continued, and Western swing even held on to its appeal. The top Western swing band was Hank Thompson and His Brazos Valley Boys, and in 1952 he had his greatest hit, "Wild Side of Life," a song that contained the line "I didn't know God made honky tonk angels." As often happens in country, a song answering another was written. It was Kitty Wells's "It Wasn't God Who Made Honky Tonk Angels":

> From the start most ev'ry heart that's ever broken
> Was because there always was a man to blame. . . .
> As you said in the words of your song
> Too many times married men think they're still single
> That has caused many a good girl to go wrong.*

It was more than an annoyed female's assertion; the song and its success proved the breakthrough for women singers in country. Kitty Wells is another Queen of Country Music, and her successful career provided a much-needed reinvigoration of the country tradition by expanding the range of experience sung about. For too long country audiences had been numbed with tales of cheatin' and teasin' women who had been the downfall of men. No longer would the message be exclusively male.

Like Hank Williams's, Jim Reeves's popularity maintained itself after his death, and to many who have recently tuned into country, it comes as a surprise that Reeves is dead. His records are played as constantly as ever, and recently there has even been an upsurge in his popularity. In a way, his career was indicative of a transition in country, for his style altered through the years.

Reeves was born in East Texas's Panola County and his early heroes were Tex Ritter, who had been born nearby, and that inescapable figure Jimmie Rodgers. Follow-

* "It Wasn't God Who Made Honky Tonk Angels," words and music by J. D. Miller. Copyright 1952 by Peer International Corporation. Used by permission.

ing another country theme, he wanted first to be a ball-
player and even made it to a St. Louis Cardinal farm team.
But that career was cut short when he injured a leg nerve while
sliding into second base. Like Roy Acuff, Reeves turned
from baseball to music, and besides being a disc jockey, he
played guitar with pianist Moon Mullican at roadhouse dates.
In 1953 he made the hit recording "Mexican Joe," and
that led to his becoming a regular on "Louisiana Hayride."
Two years later, he became a member of Opry.

Reeves's back-up instrumentation was pure honky
tonk, and in his early years he followed Williams's fast, smart
manner. But in the late fifties, he developed an individual
style, one closer to pop. There was no calculation in this; it was

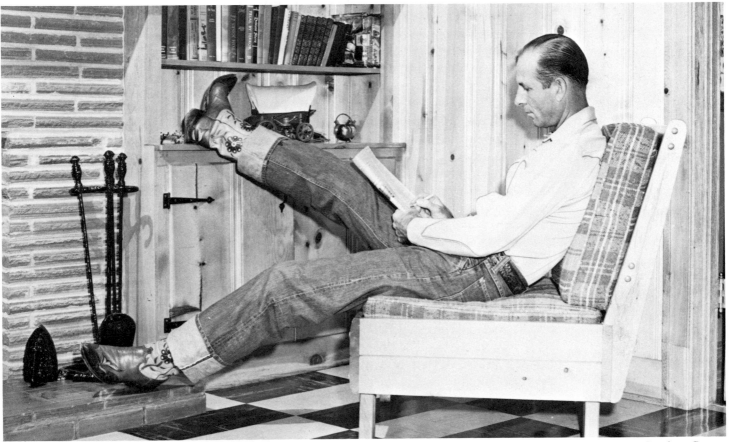

Cowboy Copas.
(Photo Gordon D.
Gillingham)

development. He worked for intimacy and smoothness, and
the way it came across was like creeping under your skin.
The hit songs kept coming: in 1957, "Four Walls," in 1959,
"Billy Bayou"; "Welcome to My World" in 1964; and
even after his death the release of tapes continued the hits:
"This Is It" in 1965; "Snow Flake" in 1966.

Reeves's manner both as a singer and as a man decided
the title his admirers gave him. He was "Gentleman Jim,"
and he was also, because of his hit "A Touch of Velvet,"
"Mister Velvet."

On July 31, 1964, just a bit over a year after the
deaths of Cowboy Copas and Patsy Cline, tragedy struck
country music again. Reeves, accompanied by his piano

95

player, Dean Manuel, was flying his own single-engine
Beechcraft Debonair from Batesville, Arkansas to Nashville.
The last message he sent was that he had just entered a
patch of heavy rain. Forty-four hours later, a rescue party
that included Eddy Arnold, Marty Robbins, and Ernest Tubb
found the wreckage in a wood patch ten miles outside
Nashville.

The citation that accompanied his posthumous election
in 1967 to the Country Music Hall of Fame took note that
Reeves was an international star, and his popularity in
England, Australia, South Africa, and the Scandinavian
countries continues to grow steadily.

Another artist who attests to the inescapable influence
of Rodgers and honky tonk is Lefty Frizzell. The height
of his popularity came in the late forties, and though
he slipped from public recognition, he remained until his
death in 1975 one of the most respected and influential
country musicians. He was born in that cradle of today's
performers, Texas, in Corsicana just south of Dallas. His
father was a driller, and the Frizzell family moved from oil
field to oil field. He grew up in the dance halls and roadhouses,
and he, too, was a sportsman—this time a teen-age boxer
who moved through the illegal club circuit. His fame came at
the same time as Williams's, with such hits as "Always Late,"
"I Want to Be with You Always," and "If You've Got
the Money, I've Got the Time." For a few months he was a
reluctant Opry regular, but he left for California and joined
the only important barn-dance radio program there,
"Compton's Town Hall Party," which also featured Ritter,
Tex Williams, Merle Travis, Freddie Hart, and a young
sideman just beginning his career, Buck Owens. It was during
that period that Frizzell would mark the direction for
another young man, Merle Haggard.

In the early fifties Frizzell recorded a tribute album to
Rodgers, one of the best of its sort, and in 1964 he made
it once again to the top of the charts with "Saginaw,
Michigan."

As Hank Williams's protégé and one-time roommate,
Ray Price, born in Cherokee County, Texas, claimed to
be a direct inheritor of Williams's style. Price, too, schooled
himself in Rodgers and Tubb, and in the singing and
playing style of Bob Wills. He had an early success with
"Don't Let the Stars Get in Your Eyes" and then followed
with "Release Me." Price took over Williams's band, the
Drifting Cowboys, and renamed them the Cherokee Cowboys.
Throughout the fifties and early sixties, Price held high the
country flame with such fine songs as Bill Anderson's
"City Lights," plus "Crazy Arms" and "Same Ole Me."

Recently, he has moved away from the Western sound
and worked closer to pop, but again it was a development
rather than a betrayal, for Price has always been an
exploratory artist. Crucial to this alteration is the recording

he made in 1963 of Hank Cochran's "Make the World Go Away," now a country classic. It is a song, and a performance, that manages the feat of being blues, country, and pop, without diluting or disgracing any of those elements.

Louisiana's Webb Pierce is another who established a major country career during the supposed doldrums in the country-music field. He has chalked up the astonishing record of seventy hits, both as a singer and a writer. Flashy dresser with a coin-studded, gaudily decorated car that has become his emblem, Pierce has a loyal following that responds to his basically honky-tonk approach. He never lets one forget he is the country boy made good, and he says his song "There Stands the Glass" ("fill it to the brim") is the national anthem of barroom songs. It is his most frequently requested number, with "Back Street Affair" a close second. All one needs to do is add that in the fifties he revived Rodgers's "In the Jailhouse Now," and one can see that Pierce knows just what his audience wants. It is what is thought of as typical country, touching the basic themes: drinking, cheating, jail. Pierce's achievement has not been in the breaking of new ground but in the accurate gauging and definition of the needs of the most entrenched country audience.

George Jones.

The news of the breakup of the marriage of George Jones and Tammy Wynette in 1975 rocked Nashville, for they were the most prominent of country-music couples, each with successful careers of their own. In fact, for a time they served as Nashville's version of Elizabeth Taylor and Richard Burton, with tales spread of their battles and reconciliations, and then again they were heralded as "the ideal couple."

Jones has often complained that country music's identity has been sullied and he has every right to be an authority; all his credentials are in order, and so is his artistry. The son of a log-truck driver, Jones was born (you guessed it) in East Texas, in Saratoga to be exact, though much of his youth was spent in Beaumont. That he made the best use of the musical influences around him is attested to in this description by Bill C. Malone in his book *Country Music U.S.A.*: "Jones' voice sometimes takes on the wailing quality of Roy Acuff or the plaintive tone of Hank Williams, and he occasionally lets his voice slide and bend around notes in a manner reminiscent of Lefty Frizzell. . . ." In addition to these, Jones himself adds as major influences Bill Monroe and Ernest Tubb.

After serving in the Marine Corps during the Korean War, Jones started his career in Beaumont saloons, and in 1954 began recording for Starday Records, a company owned by H. W. "Pappy" Dailey and Jack Starnes. Dailey later became Jones's personal manager and producer, and Jones credits him with directing his career.

His recordings number well over four hundred, with

eighty-two albums to his credit, and many of them are duets, most importantly with Margie Singleton, Gene Pitney, Melba Montgomery (especially with the "cheatin' " songs "We Must Have Been Out of Our Minds" and "Let's Invite Them Over"), Brenda Carter, and Tammy Wynette.

Jones's intense, emotional delivery has distinguished all his renditions, from his first hit "Why Baby Why" through songs like "Just One More," "White Lightning," "She Thinks I Still Care," "Things Have Gone to Pieces," and "Walk Through This World With Me."

Jones became an Opry regular for the second time in 1973, but he is evidence of an artist who didn't need that organization to become a superstar.

Nashville and records tempered the untamed, raw, cutting honky-tonk sound, and as most of the performers discussed above grew, they moderated their styles. When country music started its greatest period of popularity in the mid-sixties, though, it was the direct, unvarnished vitality of honky tonk that appealed to the new audience. For many performers the raucousness and blatantcy seemed a dead end, and one alternative was to capture a bit of the smoothness and technical felicities of pop. Country-pop had been a lively alternative for a long time, but now it had acquired respectability.

There were other performers who saw that the better course would be to carry forward honky tonk and Western

Jimmie Davis. (Courtesy Country Music Foundation Library and Media Center)

Webb Pierce. (Courtesy Roger Schutt)

swing, to make the attempt to update these root forms—
for the roots were what they had now become. Little wonder
that the base for this variety of country was once again
Texas. The most famous artists in this drive are the two
renegades Waylon Jennings and Willie Nelson.

The most dramatic instance of an artist struggling to
find his proper voice, his proper style, is that of Willie
Nelson. Nelson gained his early training in Fort Worth dance
halls. Since then, he has gone through so many changes
that those who discover him now think that he has been driven
to find a success that has eluded him unfairly. A long-time
Nelson fan will tell you that the truth is that Nelson
threw away any number of moments of success because he
is a restless, dissatisfied artist.

Nelson's distinctiveness is in his meticulous control
over the musical phrasing—almost to the point where it
sounds affected. Phrases are grouped, with slight extra pauses
between so that the following phrase is slightly rushed, with
notes held to sharpness for dramatic effect. The emphasis
is all done musically with only the merest touch of expressive-
ness. He holds his audience with a dramatic opening statement,
and then maintains suspense by holding off the inevitable
burst of the repeat. The message of the song is like a sharp
retort in a debate.

Nelson, after selling his song "Family Bible," came to
Nashville in the late fifties to write and perform. He wrote
some of his finest songs, like "Night Life," for Ray Price, but
he had written his best song two years before, a raw nerve
of pain called "Hello Walls":

Hello ceiling, I'm gonna stare at you awhile,
You know I can't sleep, so won't you bear with me awhile?
We must all pull together or else I'll lose my mind,
'Cause I've got a feelin' she'll be gone a long, long time.*

Quickly, Nelson established himself as a "master," for
he not only knew the honky-tonk style, but he treated it as
an art form. It was his sure touch and the aura of authority
that thrilled his audience. One of those schooled with Nelson
was his drummer, Johnny Bush, who went on to establish
his own career.

But by the mid-sixties, it was clear that Willie Nelson
was not sharing in the country-music boom, and that all
the "action" was going elsewhere, to such figures as Johnny
Cash, who had an eclectic style, or to Buck Owens, who
was having success with a soft-country sound. So Nelson left
Nashville, and also discarded his rather square look, let
his hair grow long, dressed like a Western hippie, and
supercharged his music so that it was abrasive, eccentric,
as difficult as modern jazz, and was precisely what pleased
him. He became "Wild Willie" instead of "Wee Willie."

Kinky Friedman, Willie Nelson, Panama Red, and, extreme right, Buck Wilkins.

Kinky Friedman.

Billy Joe Shaver.

And he returned to Texas, now a musical innovator. What Nelson knew was that country musicians were well aware of his worth, and he had to settle into a place where musical values were of more weight than financial success.

By this act of rebellion—continual musical experiment, a dramatic alteration in his dress and appearance, a rejection of Nashville—Nelson became the first revolutionist of the present country era. Someone so sure of this "message" could not help but be an example to restless others, like Kris Kristofferson (born in Brownsville, Texas), Waylon Jennings (from Littlefield, Texas), and Jerry Jeff Walker.

An important annual country-music event is Nelson's Fourth of July Picnic. His day-long festival has featured Country's rebels, Kristofferson, John Prine, Leon Russell, Billy Joe Shaver, Waylon Jennings and his wife Jessi Colter, and also gives the more staid, like Charlie Rich and Tom T. Hall, a chance to cut up a bit.

Like many of his compatriots, Waylon Jennings was schooled in honky tonks, with his father, a guitarist, as his teacher. At twelve he became a disc jockey, and two years later in Lubbock he joined up with Buddy Holly as a bass player. That was full-fledged rock-and-roll, but these Texas boys never settled for such clean-cut definitions, and to this day, Waylon insists he was always doing his own thing, and his own thing is country, no matter what the beat or the instruments. He's a country boy, and whatever song

Willie and Tracy Nelson.

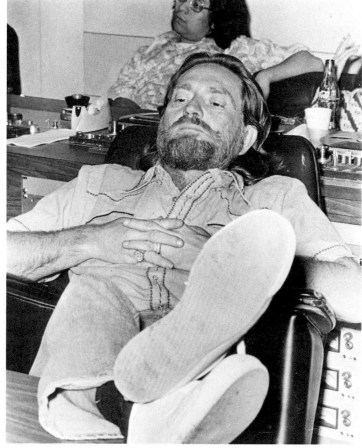

Willie Nelson.

102

he sings, it will come out country. He is dead right when he says it isn't his style that has changed, but rather there has been a relaxation of the "rules," resulting in a more inclusive definition of what the country sound is and can be.

When Buddy Holly died in 1959, his group, the Crickets, broke up and Waylon set off on his own path and formed his group, the Waylors. Chet Atkins signed them to record for RCA in 1965, and Waylon moved to Nashville, a town then very much concerned with the Nashville sound, which had little to do with the stomping, driving rhythms and assorted rock and soul that was Waylon's extension of honky tonk.

Something of a wild man, he found his match in Johnny Cash, and they spent two years breaking down doors, smashing up houses, fishing, disappearing together. Needless to say, the Nashville establishment shook their heads in pained dismay and secret glee at this appearance of headlong self-destructiveness. But that same wild, bad-boy image served to pull together an audience who long had had a fondness for antiheroes. While Waylon Jennings seemed to be bombing out in Nashville, he was also becoming an antiestablishment hero. The Texas boy was mining the new cowboy image, and his popularity forced the Nashville music community to revise its opinion of Waylon. He had won, and he claims the victory.

Waylon's most famous album, "Honky-Tonk Heroes," is devoted to the songs of Billy Joe Shaver, a Waco boy who has been a cowhand, worked in a sawmill, and who came under the influence of Willie Nelson. Shaver's tribute to Nelson says:

> Willie, you're wild as a Texas blue norther,
> Ready-rolled from the same makings as me . . .

With Nelson's encouragement, Shaver went to Nashville, and was immediately recognized as one of the wild ones, and something of a genius of a writer, with his songs recorded by Tom T. Hall, Johnny Rodriguez, Dottie West, and Bobby Bare. A few years ago he gave country a tremor by writing and singing its first song about an interracial affair, "Black Rose."

When country music is sneered at for being lily white, three names are cited in response: Charley Pride (black), Johnny Rodriguez (Chicano), and Kinky Friedman (Jewish). The last two are Texans, and though it would be straining themes a bit to see them as inheritors of the honky-tonk tradition, a case could be made for Texas breeding mavericks who give energy and vitality to standard country.

Grandpa Jones.

6
Bluegrass and the Appalachian Heritage

Sitting around backstage at the Opry or some civic auditorium waiting to go on, country-music people like to poor-mouth, to tell each other how poor their families were, how cold the winters, how bad the crops, how little they had to wear, how long they had to shovel coal to buy their first guitar. The whole series of stories, true and half-true, is told from beneath a 10X Stetson with a tooled silver band; the gesturing hands emerge from a thousand-dollar Nudie outfit, the boots propped on the make-up stand are patent-leather confections. After the tales are told, the boots carry them out onto the stage to sing and be applauded, and then off to the custom bus with the round bed and the Mediterranean decor.

These stories are built of truths, legends, sad romances, but the present is such a dim reflection of that part-remembered, part-invented time that there is a constant need to reidentify with a real past.

Some of the most important people in country have

spent their lives and careers preserving old—particularly Appalachian—musical styles, sheltering from outside influences not only the music but its way of life as well.

For generations, a rich and abundant fund of traditional music had been handed down from father to son and mother to daughter as a natural part of everyday life, lore as practical and necessary as hunting or weaving. There were lullabies, story-songs or ballads, hymns, work songs, and nonsense rhymes to liven up a play-party or a quilting bee. The instruments were traditional, most often passed along as one of few family treasures; and the voices were untrained, sometimes badly off-key, but always capable of deep emotion.

Inevitably, commercialization changed everything. New songs, more or less imitative of the old standards, had to be written to maintain an ever-changing repertoire of material before the buying public; new instruments began cropping up in country bands; big-band arrangements and modern recording techniques took away all the hard edges and imperfections; boots were cleansed of mud and dung and overalls were exchanged for tailored clothes and Western hats. And all the barns and parlors and front porches were abandoned for auditoriums, fairgrounds, and night clubs.

Nor were the changes all regrettable. Attention and support were given where they had been absent before and wonderful hybrid forms of country music developed, good songs were written, fortunes were made and an extremely lucrative recording industry grew up in Nashville. As a result, country music's wide-ranging appeal is unparallelled by any other form of entertainment. Where the music extends from the smoothness and urbanity of Eddy Arnold to the unamplified slapstick of Gid Tanner's Skillet Lickers, everybody finds something to like.

Most performers betray a mixture of traditional and liberal attitudes towards their heritage. Dolly Parton, for example, sings and writes in a nearly pure Appalachian mode, at the same time affecting an exaggerated personal appearance—massive amounts of cosmetics, elaborate hair pieces, strange pink and electric yellow outfits. "I was so poor when I was growing up," Dolly explains, "that now I want to cover myself in rich things." So, the sequins and the artifice and the bright colors have come to symbolize for Dolly and many other country performers the ease and luxury they never had as youngsters. Yet Dolly's musical style remains nearly unchanged. To hear her sing "Jolene" or "Down From Dover" is unforgettable because the music is genuine. Her style is pure, but other performers, eager to escape their background and all of its connotations—including the music—have changed their style, perhaps because anything purely "country" is too strong a reminder of wholly unglamorous times past. There is nonetheless a clear pride in having just survived the hardships of their youths and there is sweetness in the memories of families whose love made the deprivations less terrible (listen to Loretta Lynn's "Coal-Miner's Daughter").

Still there is a nagging fear that they'll wake up one morning to find themselves penniless in a shack out in the country. Which brings up a crucial point—for country people, there is no romance to country living ("there ain't nothing pretty about having a mule fart in your face"). The land, nature, the primitive quality of life, even the air are hostile when you're poor. "We were share-croppers," Grandpa Jones says. "One winter, nineteen twenty-five or 'six, all we had to eat was parched corn and sweet milk. We had a corncrib and a cow. That's all." All of which helps to explain the avid taste that once-poor people have for the trappings of a movieland picture of splendor and that seem to many others gaudy and tasteless.

In certain regions of the country though, there remains a concern for traditions, along with a concern for traditional musical standards. Old music as well as an entire, generation-old way of life is clung to in Appalachia. Change is slowest to occur there, and acceptance by outsiders is not much sought-after.

Artists like Grandpa Jones, Mac Wiseman, and others have, by their adherence to the old styles, maintained an unquestioned pride in their heritage. And many of them come from Appalachia.

Bill Monroe.

Too often these old styles are called by the grab-bag name "bluegrass," but the term is misleading since it only came into general use in the mid-fifties, out of deference to Bill Monroe, whose band was named the Blue Grass Boys, although Bill was not from the bluegrass region of Kentucky but from Rosine. Since then, the term has been used with such frequency and looseness that it has come to designate just about any music featuring a banjo or fiddle.

"Bluegrass" is accurately descriptive of the music of Bill Monroe and of his obvious disciples and followers, including certain members of his group who later formed their own bands—among them Flatt and Scruggs and Mac Wiseman. It is not accurate to connect bluegrass with artists such as Grandpa Jones, who never played for Bill Monroe, nor with David "Stringbean" Akeman, who did. Nor does it describe the recent music of the Earl Scruggs Revue, vastly different from the style of Flatt's and Scrugg's Foggy Mountain Boys, which definitely was "bluegrass."

Perhaps the term "Appalachian heritage," more general in its connotations, would be more descriptive. The songs of the Appalachian heritage are usually old standards like "Rosewood Casket," "Liza Jane," "Cotton-eyed Joe," "Poor Ellen Smith," "John Brown," and "Shady Grove." Some of these songs, "Barbara Allen" for one, date back to Elizabethan times. New songs are occasionally admitted into the fold if they are good enough—songs written by the Carters and Stonemans, songs like Bill Monroe's "Uncle Pen" and

"Crossing the Cumberlands," even one called "Jenny Jenkins," cowritten by father-and-son musicologists John and Alan Lomax (with Estil and Orna Ball), to mention only a few. "Authentic" songs, for that matter, are still being written— "Baby-O" by Jimmie Driftwood is a fine example. Driftwood (who is not actually from Appalachia but rather from Arkansas) also wrote "The Battle of New Orleans." But up to the time folk music began to be mass-marketed, there was really no need for new material. If good new songs presented themselves, fine. But the heritage was rich enough as it was.

In mountain music the voice was rarely considered a virtuoso instrument; it was simply used as another sound-producing tool. Its function was to "say" the song—the gist of

The Original Blue Grass Boys: Art Wooten, Bill Monroe, Cleo Davis, Amos Garen. (Courtesy Les Leverett)

which was thoroughly familiar to virtually everyone—usually in heavily accented mountain dialect, and to provide three-, four- and five-part harmony.

The traditional instruments of the Appalachian heritage are never amplified, and stringed instruments are predominant: guitar, bass fiddle (the bow was not used), mandolin, banjo (four- and later five-string), dulcimer (the strings are strummed with a goose-quill), autoharp (Pop Stoneman and Maybelle Carter immediately come to mind), fiddle and, sometimes, dobro. There are almost no wind instruments except rarely used accordions, celestinas, and the like, homemade panpipes, and, more recently, harmonicas. Bass and guitar ordinarily provide percussion, although in the last several years, a snare drum and brush have been admitted (without trap-sets and cymbals) for breakneck 4/4 hoe-downs and instrumentals. Piano is seldom used—it was too bulky and heavy to lug around in the mountains.

The fiddle emerged early as an instrument which encouraged great individual skill and technical virtuosity; and today, it is an integral part of country music. Good fiddling is still highly regarded. There are many outstanding fiddle players in country music today, all of them owing much of their art to the Appalachian heritage—Shortly Lavender, Johnny Gimble, Lisa Silver, the incredible Vassar Clements, Buddy Spicher, and the everlasting Fiddlin' Sid Harkreader, to name a few.

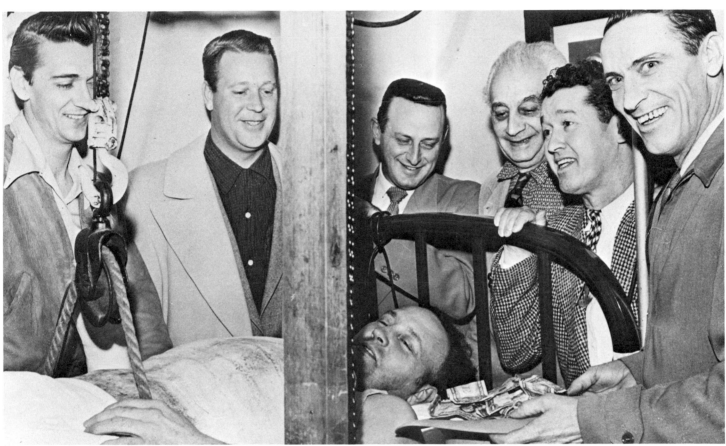

Curiously enough, the banjo was ignored as a lead instrument in serious music until 1945, the year Earl Scruggs joined Bill Monroe. Up until that time, the banjo had been used mainly in connection with comedy and novelty acts and as rhythm background in ensemble: for example in Mainer's Mountaineers, the Stanley Brothers, Gid Tanner's Skillet Lickers, Al Hopkins's Buckle Busters, the Piedmont Log Rollers, and Charlie Poole's North Carolina Ramblers.

Eminent banjo stylists, who deserve but have yet to enjoy the fame of Scruggs or John Hartford, are Stringbean Akeman, who came to the Blue Grass Boys in 1942 only to play rhythm; Grandpa Jones; Clarence Ashley, a close friend of Roy Acuff's from the time Roy came to Doc Hower's

In the early fifties Monroe was in a serious auto accident, and here is visited by an Opry crew: from left to right, Carl Smith, Eddie Hill, Jim Denny, Vito Pellettieri, Roy Acuff, Ernest Tubb. (Courtesy WSM)

Medicine Show until Ashley's death in 1967; Buell Kazee, an Elizabethan scholar and minister who recorded such old songs as "Lady Gay" (a variant of "The Wife of Usher's Well") and "Wagoner's Lad," Uncle Dave Macon, Dock Boggs, who quit the banjo to please his wife, only to pick it up again after forty-one years of coal mining; Cousin Emmy; Molly O'Day; Snuffy Jenkins, whose banjo-picking technique is similar to Scruggs's and who is from the same area in North Carolina.

But, of these masters of the banjo, it is Grandpa Jones who has lasted longer than anyone, including Earl Scruggs.

Born in Henderson County, Kentucky, Grandpa has been in show business since 1929, when he won fifty dollars in ten-dollar gold pieces in a contest sponsored by Wendell Hall in Akron, Ohio. Soon, he was a regular on Akron stations WFJC and WJW. By 1935, he had a job with Bradley Kincaid in West Virginia. "Bradley used to sing 'Barbara Allen' every night on his radio show. I learned that and 'Brown Girl and Fair Ellen' and a lot more from him."

But it was 1937 before Grandpa became interested in banjo. "Up to then, I played guitar. Then, I met Cousin Emmy who taught me how to play the style I have now. It's called the 'drop-thumb' style, where the thumb drops from the first and second down to the fifth string. You get a different sound that way. String [Stringbean] used to pluck the strings high up on the frets with the fingers of his left hand to get something like the same sound, but not quite."

In 1946, Grandpa joined the Opry and a year later he recorded "Old Rattler" for King Records in Cincinnati. That was his first hit.

Besides "Rattler," Grandpa wrote "Eight More Miles to Louisville," which was a big record for both himself and Mac Wiseman, and he also wrote "Falling Leaves" for Porter Wagoner.

Grandpa has gotten a lot of national attention due to his appearance on the TV show, "Hee Haw." There he sometimes plays duets with another fine banjoist, Roni Stoneman, as well as his solos and his comedy spots with Minnie Pearl. In their wisdom, the producers of "Hee Haw" have seen fit to discontinue his rhyming menus in answer to the question, "What's for supper, Grandpa?"

During his close to fifty years as a professional musician, Grandpa Jones has remained true to his Appalachian roots, writing songs consistent with the old style and recording many authentic mountain ballads. He and his wife Romona, who sometimes accompanies him on fiddle, live on a farm near Nashville. His name is even listed in the phonebook.

As well as anyone in country music, Grandpa Jones represents everything that the Appalachian heritage stands for, both in his music and in his life.

The Appalachian heritage owes more to Bill Monroe

than to any other single person because it was Monroe and his influence, through the Blue Grass Boys, and through graduates of this band—among them Lester Flatt, Earl Scruggs, Mac Wiseman, Don Reno, Jimmy Martin, and Sonny Osborne—that a general resurgence of interest in mountain music was born. By the late fifties, the media decided that a movement was afoot and dubbed it "bluegrass" in honor of Monroe. As we have noted, the term has been misused lately, but nevertheless, a great number of musicians who are part of the general Appalachian heritage may be more particularly identified with "bluegrass" because of their close affinity for the style developed by Monroe.

Bill Monroe's early music teachers included his mother, who died when he was ten, a black man named Arnold Schultz, his Uncle Pen, and Jimmie Rodgers, whom he knew only through records. In 1936 Bill and his brother Charlie began recording for the old Bluebird label as the Monroe Brothers. Bill formed his own Blue Grass Boys in 1938 and the following year joined the Opry. The original Blue Grass Boys included Cleo Davis, Art Wooten, and Amos Garin. But it was not until 1945, when a young banjoist from Flint Hill, North Carolina, named Earl Scruggs joined the group, that the sound later to be called bluegrass took shape.

The musical style properly identified as bluegrass differs in certain ways from the larger Appalachian heritage. Monroe's own high-pitched, nasal voice set an immediate standard; some current bluegrass vocalists have extended this quality to such a degree that the resultant whine is so mannered that it is almost incomprehensible. Secondly, Monroe's own highly sophisticated mandolin technique became a standard much imitated but rarely realized by later enthusiasts. Finally, Earl Scruggs's ingenious addition of a three-finger-roll technique of banjo picking set the final standard for "pure" bluegrass.

Bill Monroe is a proud, in many ways an unapproachable, man. He speaks of his descent from President James Monroe, and he still farms with a mule and plow. He is absolutely intolerant of carelessness or laxity in musicianship, a quality that has made him a most effective if autocratic teacher for those who have worked for him. He was elected to the Country Music Hall Of Fame in 1970.

Two distinguished graduates of the Blue Grass Boys are Earl Scruggs and Lester Flatt, who, after three years with Monroe, quit to form their own band, the Foggy Mountain Boys. The group included Jimmy Shumate on fiddle, Cedric Rainwater on bass, and Mac Wiseman on guitar. The mandolin was dropped as an instrument, Buck Graves's dobro was added and by 1955, when the Foggy Mountain Boys joined the Opry, the sound that had been "pure" bluegrass had undergone profound change.

In following years, Flatt and Scruggs, under the

sponsorship of the flour-manufacturer Martha White Mills, played almost every village and metropolis in America, featuring such perennial favorites as "Foggy Mountain Breakdown" (currently called "The Theme From *Bonnie and Clyde*"), "Roll In My Sweet Baby's Arms," and "The Ballad of Jed Clampett."

In 1969, after enjoying the adulation of the folk boom of the sixties, Flatt and Scruggs parted ways under a cloud of mystery. The gossip ran hot and heavy for a while, but, whatever precipitated the breakup, it was musically inevitable for Lester Flatt had grown conservative, while Earl Scruggs was becoming more and more experimental.

Flatt, still one of the finest singers in country music, continues to tour and play the Opry with the Nashville Grass, and is a favorite at Bean Blossom, Bill Monroe's annual bluegrass festival held in Indiana. But while there is still his benevolent interest in young musicians, something of his old fire has diminished.

Scruggs, bolstered and continually refreshed by his sons' inventiveness, is allowing the Earl Scruggs Revue to explore new horizons. New instruments, amplification, bold new songs, in opposition to the tight strictures of pure Appalachian music, abound in this group. Whether or not this freedom will result in anything but an excellent musical education for Scruggs's sons and a whole lot of fun for everybody has yet to be determined.

Earl Scruggs, after thirty years in the business, seems less concerned to preserve anything in a historical or cultural sense than to discover his own personal limits as a musical technician. What he has done is break through

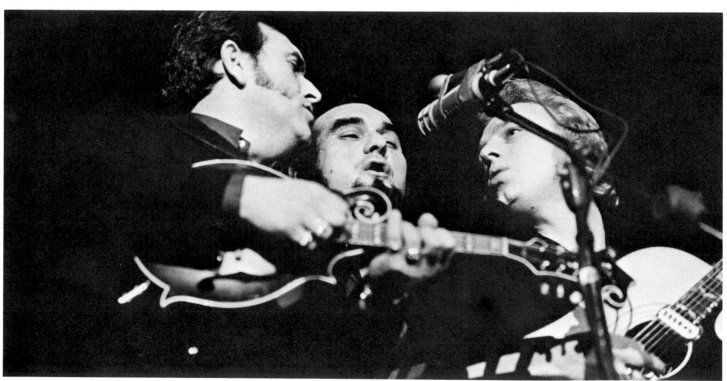

The Osborne Brothers.

112

the cloister that is Appalachian music into a never-never land of free-form jazz fantasies on Appalachian themes. Vassar Clements is doing something marginally similar with his fiddle. If Scruggs or Clements succeed, they will bring a whole new dimension to the Appalachian heritage.

The great interest in folk music during the sixties swung slowly full-circle back to country music. While in the early years the focus was more or less on Pete Seeger, Woody Guthrie, and the emergence of Bob Dylan, Joan Baez, and groups like the Kingston Trio, it was the late sixties and early seventies that Bill Monroe, Flatt and Scruggs and others were sought after like demigods and Nashville became Parnassus. For a while, if you were a bright new recording act that claimed a trendy link with the Appalachian heritage, it was the thing to do to have Earl Scruggs pick or the Carters sing harmony on your album.

The survival of mountain music, its brush with extinction, and its slow climb back into prominence, partially capped by the story of bluegrass, shows how the evolution of musical forms comes about. It also demonstrates the futility of attempting to describe in absolute terms what the elements of bluegrass are, because once described by reference to the musical style of Bill Monroe, the father of bluegrass, some one like Earl Scruggs or Jim and Jesse McReynolds or Jimmy Martin will appear to alter the form by his own inventiveness, just as Monroe himself altered the music he was extending. Finally, one is reduced to coining words like "newgrass" and "oldgrass" to deal with changes within bluegrass, which in turn is only a part of the music of our Appalachian heritage.

Earl Scruggs.

Mac Wiseman.

Country music is like a river that changes every time it rains, but a sudden deluge brings different changes. When the pressures of commercialization developed, mountain music ran the risk of either going under and being entirely forgotten, or, nearly as bad, of being swollen beyond recognition by new (polluting) influences. The people who have loved our traditions and tried so desperately to keep them intact knew all along that change would happen. But they also knew that with the proper care of a conservative attitude, change could at least be slowed down and quality preserved.

It took strength and discipline to do the job. And happily for our Appalachian heritage, there were people like Grandpa Jones and Bill Monroe.

At Mac Wiseman's Renfro Valley Bluegrass Festival.

And Mac Wiseman, too.

In recent years, bluegrass festivals have popped up everywhere, from Smokey Green's, near Lake George, New York, to the Culpepper Bluegrass Festival in Virginia; and from Bean Blossom to Mac Wiseman's Bluegrass Festival in Renfro Valley, Kentucky.

Mac, who is from Crimora, in Virginia's Shenandoah Valley, is as good on records and radio as he is in person at Renfro Valley. He's been around. After a time with Molly O'Day's band, he joined Scruggs's and Flatt's newly formed Foggy Mountain Boys, which was followed by an apprenticeship with Bill Monroe. Mac's effortless tenor voice has resulted in a series of important records including "Tis Sweet

To Be Remembered," "Wildfire," "Eight More Miles To Louisville," "I Wonder How The Old Folks Are At Home," and "When The Roses Bloom Again."

But the Renfro Valley festival, held annually the second weekend in July in Rockcastle County, Kentucky, reveals more of Mac Wiseman than anything else.

Even though he's succeeded in losing over a hundred pounds, Mac is still as imposing as Henry the Eighth; and at Renfro Valley, he is indeed a kind of royalty, strolling among his subjects as they sprawl on the grass in front of the flatbed truck that serves as a stage. Children play in packs, like forest creatures, running shirtless through the trees that encircle the long valley as their parents watch and listen and drift in the heat of a fresh new summer. It is not in steel and concrete auditoriums, but among green hills and muddied feet that Appalachian music is most at home.

As Mac leans on an open car door and smokes a fat cigar, ruminatively rolling it about in his mouth, he watches the Osborne Brothers mount the stage. With a mild joke as a sequel of feedback drives through the khaki speakers mounted on poles, the Osborne Brothers commence their tight and disciplined crooning to murmurs of applause for the very familiarity and timelessness of that sound. People come and go, folding up their blankets and deck chairs, gathering the thermos jug and the dog and the empty red Coca-Cola cups as the day moves on. The sun shines and people move back

into the trees for lunch while corn is shucked for the evening's feast. It had rained the day before, so shoes and cuffs are muddy.

Sheriff Manuel Shepard looks benignly upon the scene. "This is about the biggest thing that happens in Rockcastle County. Oh, every now and then, there's a killing, but we always know who done it. Or you get a drunk driver now and then. That's about it."

During the fiddling contest, young boys hoist themselves up to sit on the edge of the stage and swing their legs just inches from the sweating, straining fiddlers. Shige, a Japanese boy, wins applause and lazily nods as he walks off, rubber-kneed and panting, but careful to fold his hundred dollar check for second prize exactly in half. He is tickled to present his elaborate autograph to a woman with an Instamatic camera. She asks him questions very slowly as if that will make him understand. Shige just smiles.

For a mile or more down the valley behind the stage area, campers have been lining up for three solid days, according to Sheriff Shepard. With many vehicles bearing Ohio and Indiana plates, they are parked in strict diagonal rows as if in the motor pool of some motley army. A large American flag waves above a camper bus bearing a sign that reads "Get High On Bluegrass." CB call letters and whip antennas are everywhere.

On the tailgate of a camper truck, a girl plays mandolin while lanky boys watch. These are bluegrass people, not only listeners, but pickers as well. Everybody here plays something. One old man in a starched shirt that seems to be wearing him looks a little dazed as he examines a beautifully inlaid fiddle. Its owner chews on a straw and swears that it is a "Stradavary."

As evening draws on, folks button their shirts and roll down their sleeves against the mosquitoes that will go away as soon as it gets dark. Wood smoke helps, too, so they stand and talk around cooking fires and portable grills. And half a mile distant, Lulabelle and Scotty play the last song of the day.

The festival lasts for three days, and despite a dull rain all Saturday afternoon that drove nearly everyone but the kids into the ramshackle but covered wooden bleachers, everyone has burned necks and faces and arms below short sleeves—farmer's tans. After the final set, Mac says Goodbye and drive careful, we want you back here next year and the campers make a long, nomad's caravan down the dirt access roads and out of Rockcastle County.

Elvis! (Courtesy RCA Records)

118

7
Memphis Rebellion

With its regional
intonations and local manners, country music was not at first
intended for the whole nation, but in the late forties and
early fifties its performers yearned for a wider public, the only
audience that could ensure them solid financial success.
There was the example of Hank Williams, for one, before
them. The ambitions of country musicians had grown broader
in a new generation that felt there was not any special
benefit in remaining separate and insular. At a time when
the notion of what the whole country meant was expanding
(the whole country had gone to war and won that war and was
the greatest of all nations that ever were) there no longer
seemed any special reason to take pride in being provincial.
Nearly everyone had power, and the young wanted a power of
their own. They were swept along by a current that among
other things swamped popular music, and devastation was
wreaked both on country and the sentimental smoothness of
pop. Rock-and-roll would be the new world's beat. And
prominent among its first leaders were the good ole Southern

boys who a few years before would have been memorizing the Jimmie Rodgers songbook.

Even before Hank Williams's success, Eddy Arnold, the Tennessee Plowboy, had broken out of the strictures of country performing. He had begun by singing with Pee Wee King, and became a member of Opry in the early forties. Within a few years, he moderated his country accent, and emerged a national star with songs like "Bouquet of Roses" and "Cattle Call." During that period he was managed by Colonel Tom Parker, the man who later masterminded the career of Elvis Presley. Arnold had worked his soft baritone closer to the crooner pattern, like that of Sinatra or Perry Como—and now represented in debased form by Dean Martin. Likely to be forgotten is that "Make the World Go Away" and "What's He Doing in My World" are Eddy Arnold songs.

About the change, Arnold said, "I did it deliberately. I wanted to add the violins. I wanted to do the things that were smoother. I wanted to appeal to the broader masses of people. It's the respect. Our music had to have the respect."

Yes, the music had to have the respect, and the singers had to have the respect also.

That a basically country-bred performer had the flexibility to move into popular fields was proved also by the late Patsy Cline, a Blue Ridge Mountain girl, whose hit recording of "Walkin' After Midnight" (a song written for and rejected by Kay Starr) broke at the same moment she became an Arthur Godfrey's "Talent Scouts" winner. Nashville had already learned the lesson of adding the violins, adding the echo chamber, and stilling the pickin'.

Williams's music had been heralding something quite different from this market crossover. What was abrewing was a new sound or, rather, a new combination of old sounds.

Credit is given Bill Haley and the Comets who announced the coming with the blast of "Rock Around the Clock" (Hank's old "Move It On Over") and a Big Joe Turner blues roll called "Shake, Rattle, and Roll." In Cincinnati, a disc jockey named Alan Freed dubbed this hybrid of blues and country, white and black, "rock-and-roll" and that section of it which became an unwanted section of country was called "rockabilly."

The folks at Opry didn't know what was happening to them: they did know that young people couldn't have cared less about the old-timey music and its greats. They were too busy facing west of Nashville to Memphis.

A local disc jockey there named Sam Phillips had a few years before set up his own recording studio. "It seemed to me," says Phillips, "that the Negroes were the only ones who had any freshness left in their music, and there was no place in the South where they could go to record. The nearest place where they made so-called race records which was soon to be called rhythm and blues was Chicago, and most of

Eddy Arnold.

them didn't have the money or time to make the trip to Chicago."* At first, Phillips sent off his tapes to Chess Records for pressing and distribution, but in 1953 he took a gamble and started his own label as an adjunct to his Memphis Recording Service. That was the beginning of Sun Records.

Phillips can be seen rightly as a pioneer and a renegade. He promoted, took chances, encouraged, followed an incredibly accurate instinct for anticipating who would make it. Those who did make it also quickly left Phillips, with some justification. Compared with the recording studios of New York, and their promotion staffs, his was a performance that verged on the amateur. That proved an advantage because his imagination and pluck were unhindered. His methods lacked finesse, high musical standards, and professional craft—all the ingredients that popular music had smothered itself to death in. The new sound was rough, and that roughness spoke for its being closer to the spirit of the youth of the country. It is remembered as the first time a popular music form was created specifically for kids; for the elders its sounds and lyrics were meaningless when they weren't outright disgusting.

Part of the peculiar vitality of American music is that its greatest artists seem to arrive full-blown and outside a tradition, but on closer scrutiny it turns out that they have combined what had seemed antagonistic traditions. It is as if our native cultural resources are nearly unending. Just when all folk sources seem to have dried up, out came Bob Dylan with a new method of phrasing and quirks of pronunciation, a whine and a meanness thinly covering sentimentality. No question about it, it was authentic, but authentic what? Not of a region, but of a pervasive and previously inarticulated attitude, and this time a national one. On examination his tunes are simple, the songs unstructured with a repetitiousness that is disguised by the phraseology, and the lyrics so simple that one is compelled to assume there is an underlying complexity. But it is his social stance and style of presentation that account for his originality, and his success. He sounds *real*, just as real as Son House, Sonny Terry, Robert Johnson, or the Carters and Jimmie Rodgers. And just as real, just as authentic in the new way, were Dylan's predecessors who were all discovered by Sam Phillips: Elvis Presley, Johnny Cash, Conway Twitty, Carl Perkins, Roy Orbison, Jerry Lee Lewis, and Charlie Rich.

All of these had the gift (and still have lively remnants of it) of being in that middle area where American audiences like to find their musical heroes: not overly schooled, close to colloquial, sincerity more visible than craft, an essence that is perceived as anarchic and rebellious.

After their lessons had been learned and they had been

* The Sam Phillips, Marion Keisler, and Elvis Presley quotes in this section are from Henry Pleasants, *The Great American Popular Singers*, (New York: Simon & Schuster, 1974), pp. 264, 265, 267.

imitated, their once astonishing and relieving originality is flattened out, bleached. Absorbed, it has entered the broader history. Elvis Presley has become comfortably old-hat, and his tours occur with the same regularity as those periodic revivals of *Gone With the Wind*; the image stretched out, the sound overhauled, still a lot of fun but disconcertingly and sadly antique.

In East Tupelo, Mississippi, Elvis Presley had his first exposure to music, and that music was white gospel music at the Assembly of God church:

"We used to go to these religious singin's all the time. There were these singers, perfectly fine singers, but nobody responded to them. Then there were the preachers, and they cut up all over the place, jumpin' on the piano, movin' ever' which way. The audience liked them."

When the Presleys moved to Memphis, Elvis listened to Acuff and Tubb on the radio; he also listened to another station that was not broadcasting for the whites, and he heard the music of B. B. King and Muddy Waters.

Patsy Cline's boot, at Ryman Auditorium.

"I'd play along with the radio or phonograph, and taught myself the chord positions. We were a religious family, going around together to sing at camp meetings and revivals, and I'd take my guitar along with us when I could. I also dug the real low-down Mississippi singers, mostly Big Bill Broonzy and Big Boy Crudup, although they would scold me at home for listening to them. 'Sinful music,' the townsfolk in Memphis said it was. Which never bothered me, I guess . . ."

In 1953, then a truckdriver and sometime entertainer, he went to the Memphis Recording Service to cut a record for himself. Phillips wasn't around at the time and Marion Keisler, the office manager, was the one who listened to him sing. After the first chorus, she rushed to find a scrap of tape so that her boss could hear this boy.

"The reason I taped Elvis was this: Over and over I remember Sam saying, 'If I could find a white man who had the Negro sound and the Negro feel, I could make a billion dollars.' This is what I heard in Elvis, this . . . what I guess they now call 'soul,' this Negro sound. So I taped it. I wanted Sam to know."

A year later, Presley began to record for Sun Records, and the first number was a wild version of Bill Monroe's "Blue Grass of Kentucky," threads of the bluegrass sound twined through blues. Among Presley's early hits, "Hound Dog" was a Leiber and Stoller reworking for Big Mama Willie Mae Thornton of an old blues number, and "Blue Suede Shoes" was Carl Perkins's song. Following in Williams's line, Presley appeared frequently on "Louisiana Hayride," and on the Grand Ole Opry.

To the great public, Presley was seen as a menacing, sinister force; in performance he gyrated his hips and his singing was not suggestively sexual, it was explicitly sexual. He was the counterpart of Marlon Brando in *The Wild One*—

a mumbling barbarian, causing horror and outrage, except to the girl who knows what good lurks underneath it all. His appeal, many claimed, was extramusical. It wasn't. Music had just been reinvigorated with an infusion of explicit sex. That lack of inhibition, learned from the blacks, freed and made careers for a string of Southern boys. Later, those boys would come to resent Presley and announce that they had been there first; that he was opportunistic and plagiaristic; that he sold out to Hollywood. That was the voice of envy, for Presley's success was exactly the kind they all wanted.

The person overlooked in the Presley shuffle was the writer of "Blue Suede Shoes," Carl Perkins, who also wrote "Honey Don't," "Matchbox," "Gone, Gone, Gone," and

PERSONAL MANAGEMENT CONTRACT ENTERED
INTO BETWEEN W. S. MOORE III AND
ELVIS PRESLEY

WHEREAS, W. S. Moore, III, is a band leader and a booking agent, and Elvis Presley, a minor, age 19 years, is a singer of reputation and renown, and possesses bright promises of large success, it is the desire of both parties to enter into this personal management contract for the best interests of both parties.

This contract is joined in and approved by the Father and Mother of Elvis Presley, *Vernon Presley* and *Mrs. Vernon Presley* Presley.

IT IS AGREED that W. S. Moore, III, will take over the complete management of the professional affairs of the said Elvis Presley, book him professionally for all appearances that can be secured for him, and to promote him, generally, in his professional endeavors. The said W. S. Moore, III, is to receive, as his compensation for his services, ten (10%) percent of all earnings from engagements, appearances, and bookings made by him for Elvis Presley.

IT IS UNDERSTOOD AND AGREED that this is an exclusive contract and the said Elvis Presley agrees not to sign any other contract pertaining to his professional work nor make any appearances at any time for any other person or manager or booking agent, for a period of one (1) year.

Now, we, *Vernon Presley* and *Mrs. Vernon Presley*, father and mother of Elvis Presley, join in this contract for and in his behalf, confirm and approve all of its terms and his execution of same and our signatures are affixed thereto.

The said W. S. Moore, III, agrees to give his best efforts to the promotion and success of the said Elvis Presley professionally.

SIGNED AND EXECUTED on this _12th_ day of _July_ 1954.

W. S. Moore
W. S. Moore, III

Elvis Presley
Elvis Presley

Vernon E. Presley
Father of Elvis Presley

Gladys Presley
Mother of Elvis Presley

Elvis Presley's first contract, 1954.

"All Mama's Children." On his way to New York to appear
on the Perry Como and Ed Sullivan shows, Perkins was
in a freak car accident that suspended his career just when his
recording of "Blue Suede Shoes" was taking off. It was
Presley's version that became the national hit, helped by
Presley's appearance on the Jackie Gleason show.

　　　If the intended direction was different, Perkins
followed the rutted road of many young country performers.

　　　He resumed performing some months after the
accident, but the impetus was gone, and then it became clear
that his brother Jay, who had been in the car with him,
was dying. Perkins spent the last months of his brother's life
with him, and after Jay's death Carl was overcome by a

Elvis Presley with a friend. (Courtesy Charlie Walker)

Elvis Presley and Hank Snow. (Photo Gordon D. Dillingham)

125

sense of the futility of all his efforts.

"I didn't do any work until the early part of 1959. I had spent all my money on hospital bills, and I had to go back. Then it got hard. See, I had started drinking in those honky-tonks, people would set beers on the stage saying, 'Give that Perkins boy some beer, he'll make that guitar talk!' By 1959 I was drinking heavy. When you're a country boy just months from the plow, and suddenly you're a star with money in your pockets, cars, women, big cities, crowds, the change is just too fast. You're the same person inside, but you're a star outside, so you don't know how to act. You're embarrassed about the way you talk, the way you eat, the way you look. You can't take the strain without a crutch. For me it was booze—I've seen the bottom of a lot of bottles."*

The man Perkins credits with bringing him out of that slump was another Memphis discovery, Johnny Cash, who had spent his childhood not far from where Perkins was brought up. Cash's father, Ray, was among the first to be given land in Dyess Colony, Arkansas, a cooperative funded by the Federal Emergency Relief Administration in 1934 to aid impoverished farmers.

After serving in the army in Germany, Cash moved to Memphis, and tried to earn money as a door-to-door appliance salesman while practicing his music. In those early days, Cash, Presley, and Perkins appeared together, performing on the backs of flatbed trucks. His first success came with two songs he recorded for Sam Phillips, "Hey Porter" and "Cry, Cry, Cry," still among his best compositions, and he was to have even greater success with another of his own songs, now a classic, "I Walk the Line." On these recordings he is backed by the Tennessee Two, Luther Perkins and Marshall Grant, and they gave him more than a distinctive sound: they stood by him when the tolls of unexpected success that Carl Perkins outlines began to ravage Cash. It wasn't booze for Cash; it was pills.

He drove himself to such a degree that he became a physical wreck, and the major impetus for his recovery came from June Carter, and when even her remarkable courage was exhausted, from her mother, Maybelle Carter. But during these years of agony, Cash continued to perform and record, and when he reemerged it was with a strength and control and a dramatic force that couldn't have been predicted. The albums recorded at San Quentin and Folsom prisons represent Cash at his best. Part of their power is that they capture the qualities of live performance, in which Cash is invariably better than he is in the studio. When he works live the gut feelings that he best portrays find their quickest response. The prison audience knows exactly what Cash sings about, and they inform us of his urgency and perceptiveness.

* Quoted in Michael Lydon, *Rock Folk* (New York: The Dial Press, 1971), pp. 40–41.

June Carter and Johnny Cash. (Courtesy Les Leverett)

Johnny Cash. (Courtesy Les Leverett)

Carl Perkins.

Carl Perkins.

Because of the continual curiosity about his personal life, Cash's musical accomplishment is too often left unremarked upon. At no point in his career did he cease studying, researching material, sharpening his performances, reinvigorating the materials that are country music's basis for ongoing importance. Conscientiously, he extended his range, adding to his repertoire blues, ballads, gospel, protest, Western, folk, and work songs. All this without transforming the songs to suit his personality—it was that personality that opened up to encompass the wealth of heritage. Most often his albums are centered around a theme: heroes of the old West, railroading, prison life; and this is never a gimmick, but an opportunity for him to explore the genre and revive worthy material. There have been few

Conway Twitty.

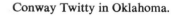
Conway Twitty in Oklahoma.

Sam Phillips of Sun Records.

Linda Gail with her brother Jerry Lee Lewis.

singers so actively appreciative of the vast inheritance of country, so capable of performing it with accuracy and adding to it with their own songs. This conscientiousness allowed him to learn the blues from the late Luther Perkins, the mountain songs from Maybelle Carter, and to include in his repertoire the compositions of young writers like Gordon Lightfoot, Dylan, Tom Paxton, and Kris Kristofferson. A short list of those songs he is identified with demonstrates this range: "Understand Your Man," "I Walk the Line," "Orange Blossom Special," "Wreck of the Old 97," "The Legend of John Henry," "Five Feet High and Rising," "The Ballad of Ira Hayes," "Sunday Morning Coming Down."

Now, with a large house overlooking Old Hickory Lake in Hendersonville, Tennessee, Cash has become one of country music's most solid citizens. He has also become an active church member, and has made a film in Israel on the life of Christ, performed for the Billy Graham crusade, fostered his image as a family man. His daughters and June's daughters have performed in his show, and a recent album cover shows him frolicking on a hill of beans with his son. Though more subdued and increasingly sentimental and without the early anguish, Cash's music has lost none of its vitality, and before an audience he remains the consummate performer. His have been rare and heroic triumphs. If he has encouraged others to see him as a worthy model, he has justification. He is a pretty good one.

Like Presley, Jerry Lee Lewis was brought up in the music and traditions of the Assembly of God church, and much of his charged performances has the fervor of hysteria. He whips the piano and his audience into a frenzy. His Louisiana roots imbued him with a broad-river streak of craziness that he shares with Cajun Doug Kershaw. The walloping that Kershaw gives his fiddle, Lewis gives his piano (they share other traits as well).

Jack Clement, then with Sun, cut Lewis's first record, "Crazy Arms" and followed it with "A Whole Lotta Shakin' Goin' On." Sexuality was so rampant on the latter record that it was given the stamp of success: it was banned from the airwaves. But nothing stills Lewis, and his national fame was made when he ripped up the stage before the television cameras on the Steve Allen Show. Quickly, hit followed hit: "Great Balls of Fire," "High School Confidential," "Breathless." In the midst of this, Lewis took as his third wife his thirteen-year-old second cousin. Of course, he hadn't bothered to divorce his first two, and the scandal it caused sunk him as a bookable performer. For almost eight years Lewis performed without recapturing that first flush success, but when everyone had thoroughly written him off and away as only a memory with which to recall the heyday of their wild youth, he delivered with a song that could only be designated true country: a real sobber about a man jilted at the last minute by a girl he has just picked up in a honky tonk, "Another Place, Another Time." From then on, Lewis was no more the rock-and-roll has-been, but a big country star. That didn't mean he felt the need to reform his wild ways; he remains unregenerate and is loved for being one of the music's bad boys.

The tale of Harold Jenkins from Friars Point, Mississippi, (forty miles from Presley's birthplace) presents us with a different kind of transformation. From the same region as the other rockabilly figures, he took a little longer finding his niche. Though he had performed as a child, it wasn't until after the army that he thought he'd try for a music career. Like Acuff and Charley Pride, he could have played professional baseball, for before being drafted he had been signed by the Philadelphia Phillies. But it was listening to Presley and Perkins that made him feel sure he could manage that kind of sound. After months of working and taping in the Sun studios, a friend of a friend suggested he come to New York and try there. In the Big City, he discarded the name Harold Jenkins and searched the map for a new one. The towns of Conway, Arkansas and Twitty, Texas gave him what he needed, and it was as Conway Twitty that he recorded for Mercury Records. Then he toured the Canadian circuit, and developed a style that he admits was close to Presley's. He returned to the South, but this time to Nashville, where he recorded "It's Only Make Believe" for MGM Records. At first, the record went nowhere, and ready to give the whole effort up Twitty went to his father-in-law's farm in Arkansas. It was there the news came to him that "It's Only Make Believe" was an overnight sensation.

For years he pursued his career as a rock-and-roll performer, but in the mid-sixties he began to yearn for something else, something different, something closer to his background. In the middle of a show in a club on the

Charlie Rich.

New Jersey coast, he made up his mind. That night he canceled the rest of his engagement, and future ones, took a plane to Nashville, and determined to begin all over again. He called his close friend, the composer Harlan Howard, and told him he was going to follow Howard's advice and go "country."

With "Next in Line," "Hello Darlin'," and duets with Loretta Lynn like "After the Fire Is Gone" and "You've Never Been This Far Before" (banned from radio in the progress of country lyrics from suggestive to frank), Twitty became a country star, his past incarnation wiped out. Today, he records with his daughter Cathy, and his son Michael Twitty, too, is establishing his own career.

The last major figure of the Memphis contingent is Arkansas-born Charlie Rich, the Gray Fox, who played backup piano on the early recordings of the Sun stars. Though he had a hit with "Lonely Worlds," his real triumphs began with Dallas Frazier's "Mohair Sam" and in 1973 he became a Triple Crown Country Music Award winner with the single and album "Behind Closed Doors." Rich is a blues singer and piano player, and his versions of Hank Williams's songs stress the blues element, but no one in present country is too concerned with such definitions. Rich lists himself in the crossover category, not by any special effort but for the best of reasons—he does what he does best.

Charlie Rich.

The revolution was over, and the counterrevolution featured the original upstarts. In some ways, the revolution had entered into a too violent phase for the performers discussed here, and also for the audience. Rock had moved into hard rock, acid rock, leaving stranded and puzzled a sizable audience who yearned for something simpler, something to hum, words that captured their feelings. What was so unendurable about rock was its sophistication, worldliness, elitism. It was terrifying to confront such jaded teen-agers, who stopped bothering about sexual identity and started taking trips of no great distance. Worse even, rock seemed irrelevant to ordinary existence and nonfunctional. By comparison, country, even with its male chauvinism, bigotry, tragic loves, sentimental deaths, and recalls to a past that never had been, seemed so decent, clear, and honest. Acid rock rebels by ignoring most typical lifestyles; country rebels with low-down women, cursing men, truckers as heroes, raunchiness, infidelity, and a general loathing of what the modern world has come to. (By the mid-seventies, a lively amalgam of folk, rock, blues, and country surfaced, offering a gutsy third way. It's featured performers are Maria Muldaur, Melissa Manchester, Janis Ian, Randy Newman, Jackson Brown, Bruce Springsteen, and Patti Smith.)

With the return of the prodigal performers and audience by the mid-sixties, Opry veterans started polishing their buttons, bows, and studs. And Nashville was no longer merely the headquarters of a regionally based music. It was the heart of the middle heart of America.

Tom T. Hall.

8
Nashville
Ascendant

It's inescapable. No matter what claims are made for Bakersfield, Memphis, Houston, or anyplace else, Nashville remains the only capital of all country music. It is the place from which it originates and the place to which its performers must return. Though Nashville's country reputation originated with the Grand Ole Opry, it is as a recording and publishing center that it retains its preeminence.

More than that, Nashville is considered the hub of middle-American popular culture, so much so that Robert Altman's movie *Nashville* used the city and the country-music business and fan populace as a metaphor for all of the United States. In the film, Nashville was peopled by those who conceived their lives in soap-opera terms, who were victimized by social forces, and most of the stars were depicted as frail or misguided innocents. Like the music (which most country artists believe was poorly captured), it celebrates the heroism of losers and martyred dupes—

and is tender yet sternly moral.

The actuality of the city comes as something of a surprise to those who have known it either as the place where Opry comes from or the overpublicized center of a major segment of the music industry.

Wealthy Nashvillians pride themselves on their culture, sophistication and the beautifully landscaped settings of their large homes. This is the city of Andrew Jackson's mansion the Hermitage, the location of Vanderbilt University, Fisk University, and a banded-together collection of colleges: Belmont, David Lipscomb, Scarritt.

At Belle Meade Country Club, Nashville's debutantes make their entrance into society at the Swan Ball. In fact,

there are few classier places than the Belle Meade section of Nashville, and for Southern grandness it has a fair claim to rival Atlanta or Savannah. At the War Memorial Auditorium (where for a brief time Opry performances were held) there are seasons of symphony and ballet. The wood replica of the Parthenon (the set of the concluding moments of the film *Nashville*) is a suggestive emblem of this city.

The country-music industry has nothing to do with this aspect of Nashville's social life. Country sits uncomfortably here. The major area of the industry is within walking distance of Capitol Hill, with its state offices, law courts, and the towers of National Life. You walk downhill from there to get to lower Broadway off which, on a sidestreet, is Ryman Auditorium, now deserted but for tourists. Lower Broadway itself is crowded with sleazy massage parlors, porno-flick houses, and music bars. Tootsie's Orchid Lounge, walls splattered with autographed photos of country musicians Tootsie bankrolled and staked in their hungry days, still remains secure across from the country eatery, Linebaugh's Restaurant, and Ernest Tubb's music-and-record shop. Like Ryman, they deserve to be designated historic sites.

Perhaps ten-minute's walk west, you pass the plush Hall of Fame Motel, where it is rumored certain stars have private suites, and where the lobby and lounge exude show-biz hustle.

Tootsie's Orchid Lounge.

A block away is the nonprofit institution from which the motel takes its name, The Country Hall of Fame and Museum (the pavement in front, like that of Hollywood Boulevard, is inscribed with the names of stars), a small but affectionate collection of memorabilia of country greats with the Country Music Foundation Library and Media Center belowstairs. In 1976 it doubled the size of its facilities. Across the street to the right is the headquarters of the Country Music Association, an organization pledged to the dissemination and protection of the business of country music. It manages the Country Music Awards, the Disc Jockey Convention, the week-long Fan Fair, provides radio stations with information, oversees copyright problems, and is amazing for its efficient promotion of an industry that is usually scattershot.

It serves as the entranceway to an area called Music Row, in appearance an unassuming middle-class neighborhood, but a neighborhood whose one-family homes have been converted into recording studios, agencies, and performers' offices, and where modern style mini-posh new buildings serve major record companies. In this one-mile-square section, all the business of country is contained.

In the suburbs of the city—such as Madison and Hendersonville—are the elaborate, sprawling homes of the stars. A tour bus will take you to them, and there is greater chance of your shaking hands or glimpsing a celebrity than if

Tootsie's Orchid Lounge.

you take a similar tour of Beverly and Hollywood Hills.

From certain hotels, you can take a bus to Opryland, where the Grand Ole Opry House now resides fourteen miles the city limits. The park is open from the spring to early fall, but the Opry House is open all year. On non-Opry performance nights, it offers touring Broadway shows or local symphony performances.

With traditional hang-out joints, bus tours, cramped business section in an urban sprawl, local version of Disneyland, museums devoted to a popular entertainment form, Nashville takes its lead from Los Angeles. And as Los Angeles is notorious for not being a moviegoing town, Nashville is not a country-music-concert town. Performers

rarely play the municipal auditorium, for they just don't draw
a substantial audience. The city seems to regard the industry as
a curiosity, and a freak one.

There are the clubs where you can hear live country,
the longest lasting is the Exit-In near Vanderbilt, where
the range is diverse and where major performers like John
Prine, John Hammond, Doctor Hook, Kris Kristofferson, as
well as Dottie West, Bobby Bare, and Shel Silverstein appear.
Off lower Broadway is the Old Time Pickin' Parlor, home of
bluegrass, featuring at times Bill Monroe, Lester Flatt, the
Misty Mountain Boys, Vassar Clements; and also near
Broadway is Possum Holler, George Jones's cavernous club.
Farther up the hill is Printers' Alley, famous both for strip

Tootsie's Orchid Lounge.

joints and music clubs. The poshest spot in town is the night
club atop Roger Miller's King of the Road Hotel.

In point of fact, Nashville's resemblance to Los
Angeles is a small-scale one. There are the hangers-on, the
young and dazzled who staff the offices, the desperate not-so-
young who feel they are constantly missing out and not
sure who to blame, a raucousness that is thinly disguised
bitterness, steady musicians who disdain the hoopla,
stars graded on a status scale: accessible, hidden, old-timey,
grand, new wealthy, over-the-hill, powerful. There is an eerie
feel that everyone is on the outside of the real action, most
because they are placed there, others because they have chosen
that safe, sane spot.

Del Reeves.
(Courtesy Top Billing)

Nashville has been becoming the Los Angeles of the East since the late fifties, and there were signs of it before then. Publishing companies and recording studios were part of the scene from early on, but the country-music boom that hit the country in the late sixties obviously affected Nashville most of all. Since then the town has become a stylish place, a mecca not only for fans but for entrepreneurs and upstarts. Every few months from 1968 through the early seventies, one national magazine after another featured lead stories on the national rage for country, and discovered in the process that Nashville existed.

For recording, Nashville had two great advantages—the well-equipped, comfortable new studios, and the backup musicians who played in a manner so distinctive that it was dubbed the Nashville Sound. Even in the early fifties, singers like Rosemary Clooney traveled down to record there, and in more recent years Joan Baez, Buffy St. Marie, Ringo Starr, Maria Oswald, Bob Dylan, and Paul McCartney have made the same journey.

The aura that the name gives brought television taping to the city. "The Johnny Cash Show" was filmed at Ryman, "Hee Haw" and "The Porter Wagoner Show" are made in Nashville. The television studios behind the Opry stage are supposedly the best in the world. From the Opry stage comes the annual presentation of the Country Music Awards, and also other country specials.

Like any other boom town, like any other American city devoted to the business of popular entertainment, Nashville seems—with its tight little offices, plastic lounges, seedy sections, bustling motels and hotels, and bevies of enthusiastic tourists—slightly crazed. Those who hope for "stardom," who adore celebrity and celebrities come across as a trifle frightening; don't they know that tomorrow morning they might wake up and find the whole business irretrievably out of date? There is the possibility that the action will move on, and those single-level bungalow offices with steeped roofs might become as empty and anachronistic as studio backlots. Still, there is the romance of the tawdry and the lost—the cosmic cowboys at the pinball machines, the country-music bums. country hustlers.

It is not a particularly distinctive characteristic that those who come to Nashville, like those who come to Los Angeles, New York, Las Vegas, have little sense of what they want except for making a hit record and being loved by audiences. Any other result is excess. It is always hard to know what to buy, what to do with money. Few who aren't born to it do know. And so it is with the young stars. The best thing is to throw it away, and that's what they do. Slightly older ones deal it out for gaudy home decoration, specially designed cars and buses; the younger ones drink or smoke it up. Those country-music tales of lives of woe have become revved up, revised for new times. The outlines of

Tompall Glaser.

Tompall Glaser, Captain Midnight at the pinball machine, Johnny Purrell.

the legends of Jimmie Rodgers (burning himself out to gather the last possible buck so that he could leave an estate), Hank Williams (dissipating it all because essentially he could only fail and anyway it was all worthless), and Johnny Cash (keep changing and pull a fast one on the devil) are all lived over and over again.

More often forgotten in the review of the biographies of the stars are the histories of those who have survived and survived well: Roy Acuff, Ernest Tubb, Hank Snow, Minnie Pearl—strong presences. Also there are those, the bulk of the Opry regulars for instance, who have never defied the gods and really attempted great success, who have worked steadily and modestly, content with what they have managed. Today's country music is not making those of that breed.

Recognizing the chanciness of the entertainment business, some have made the attempt to get into "real" businesses, the result of which is more likely to be disastrous than successful: Minnie Pearl's Fried Chicken, Conway Twitty's Twittyburgers, Roger Miller's hotel, Tex Ritter Burgers, Jimmy Dean sausage, Loretta Lynn's Westernwear stores, Eddy Arnold has considerable land holdings, Sam Phillips owns a chunk of Holiday Inn stock. It is the commercialization of the real Americana (burgers and fried chicken, land and motels, levis and leisure suits). The ambitions and lifestyles of the stars are the same as those of their audience. It is as it was before.

The much touted realism and true-to-life subject matter that is accounted the reason for country's success is precisely this mirror reflection. Country is a great American romance and self-celebration, and it isn't any more real than "Our Town." The music is reassurance that this life is worth

Hank Cochran and Jeannie Seely.

dramatizing and that it has value and point. The glamour of cheating wives, self-reliant men, tough home-loving truckers, wrong-done women, drifters, broken loves is the glamour of American ideals. We are discontent and anxious, and these feelings underpin our music. The stories and the sentiments are fakery; the need to invent them isn't.

The music itself is its own grandest feature, and it is the least remarked-on aspect. The musicianship of country is astounding, but its effect seems to be subliminal. The Nashville Sound, fostered by the admirable acumen of Chet Atkins (a master guitarist, but still more powerful as a record producer), gives Nashville a genuine prominence. Some of the local backup musicians are the most sought-after accompanists, and the main reason why singers having nothing to do with country want to record there. These musicians include artists who have made considerable successes as soloists: Charlie McCoy, pictured always with his harmonica, but also accomplished on many other instruments; on guitar, Tommy Allsup, Billy Sanford, Hank Garland, Grady Martin, Jerry Shook, Reggie Young, Jerry Kennedy; piano, Floyd Cramer, David Briggs, Pig Robbins, Bobby Emmons; fiddle, Vassar Clements, Johnny Gimble, Buddy Spicher; steel guitar, Weldon Myrick, Pete Drake, Buddy Emmons, Lloyd Green; bass, Henry Strzelecki, Norbert Putnam; drums, Buddy Harman, D. J. Fontana, Kenny Buttry, Gerry Kerrigan, Kenny Malone; vocal groups, the Jordanaires, the Nashville Edition, the Anita Kerr Singers.

All these, separately and in combination, know how to invigorate, extend, manipulate the country sound, as well as the blues, jazz, ragtime. They are masters of the best traditions of American popular music at its most engaging. It

Sonny James.

141

is polished, technically assured, eclectic. They manage a relaxed, easygoing style, enriched by the fact that they have played together for a long time, and therefore can improvise with assurance. In its earliest stage, the Nashville Sound bordered on the musically innocuous—some of the musicians played progressive jazz at late-night clubs to get away from their smooth recording renditions—but lately it has developed a stronger recall of sharper times, reflecting the popularity of country as country and not sedated for pop tastes.

Jean Shepard.
(Courtesy Top Billing)

The community of writers has grown, and within the business they are reckoned as great forces. As singers felt compelled to write their own material, some writers have felt the compulsion to perform their own songs. Among the following it is sometimes hard to make the distinction between performer and writer, or to determine which aspect is most impressive: Cash, Haggard, Willie Nelson, Roger Miller, Tom T. Hall, Kristofferson, Bill Anderson, Mickey Newbury, Mel Tillis, Dallas Frazier, Tom Glazer, Freddie Hart, Marty Robbins, Buck Owens. Then there is Presley (who wrote "Love Me Tender" and "Heartbreak Hotel"), Billy Joe Shaver, Red Simpson, Jeanne Pruett (who wrote for Marty Robbins), Jeannie Seeley (married to leading Country writer Hank Cochran, sings with Jack Greene, and has written for Dottie West, Faron Young, Connie Smith), Red Lane, Don Gibson ("I Can't Stop Loving You," "Oh Lonesome Me").

Young songwriters beef they can't get a hearing because the performers are all singing their own songs; performers feel they need to write to prove they have the qualifications for stardom.

The other dilemma is that of the crossover artist. What has the world come to if someone like John Denver, a writer for Peter, Paul, and Mary in the old days, proclaims he is a country boy walking down country roads and everyone believes him so that he even wins a Country Music Award? Especially after the previous year's award to Olivia Newton-John caused a week-long revolt? Either it means that anyone can be called country or that country is becoming obsolete as a definition. Mac Davis plays a combination of Tom Jones and Elvis, Glen Campbell makes lonesome sounds as a rhinestone cowboy, Bobby Goldsboro, Honey's widower, slips easily into a country accent, as does Ricky Nelson. While these are busy shuffling the dust off their boots so that you know their credentials, there are others like Canadian Anne Murray and North Carolinian Ronnie Milsap who take every other opportunity to say they don't like being called country because they don't want to be limited. The Country Gentleman, Sonny James, is country, but his renditions of "I'll Never Find Another You" and "A World of Our Own" or any of his successes have all the smooth characteristics of any pop song.

142

Barbara Fairchild. (Courtesy William Morris Agency)

Larry Gatlin.

Merle Haggard.

It is a nagging question, this one of definition, and will cause more arguments in Nashville than any other topic. For a time, Roger Miller, whose quirky, witty, brilliant songs brought him national attention, and which caused even *The New Yorker* to do a lengthy profile of him, was cold-shouldered in Nashville for becoming too citified. Roy Clark manages to keep his credentials intact in both worlds, but perhaps the effort has robbed his recent performances of their former vitality.

What this problem indicates is usually an uneasiness in the performer, a feeling that they aren't reaching their greatest potential audience. For the most assured of country performers, the question glides right by. Tom T. Hall is the perfect instance.

Hall, from Olive Hill, Kentucky, tells his stories in a rambling, friendly way. He never lets himself get wrought up or outright angry, though his listeners feel the tension of his restraint. With that wry, dry approach characteristic of country, he keeps his distance and his firm, slightly distancing identity. There is much in his manner that is like that of the cracker-barrel philosopher. He sidesteps sentimentality, even in an archly simple number like "I Love," and that's one of the reasons his song "Homecoming" (in which on a brief visit home he tells his dad what he has been doing since they last saw each other), is one of his most moving. Pervasive through the song, but never articulated, is the fact that the son cannot make his world comprehensible to the father; there is only the loving, doomed attempt.

Both the stories and the way he tells them seem familiar because they have the immediate feel of truth, but that is all craft and a special genius. Hall deflates self-importance, and the joke is often at his own expense. The themes are often about luck, chance, the effect of circumstance beyond our control. They assume we are all well-meaning (you wouldn't fool around with someone if you had first known they were married; when you find out, it is too late), we appreciate forthrightness and candor and happy people.

In one of his best, "Week in a Country Jail," he tells of being arrested for speeding. During his one-week term, he gets bologna and eggs every day, and by the end of the week even the jailer's wife is looking good. Having gone slightly crazy, he invites her to run off with him. The situation is slight, but it is sufficient pretext for the details, which are both absurd and correct.

He sings gospel ("Me and Jesus"), does straight blues ("That's How I Got to Memphis"), defends those who ruffle hypocritical morality ("Harper Valley PTA"), is a caustic social observer ("I Washed My Face in the Morning Dew"), evokes Dixieland ("I Want to Hear It Again"), but it is as a narrator of modern life that he is at his best. When he sang of Vietnam or of a brush with a switchblade in a German bar, he stretched the themes of country, but his method is country at its purest. In interviews he mentions Hemingway as his favorite writer, but in his own manner he resembles Twain.

Merle Haggard is another instance of a fiercely independent artist and of one who is an exemplar of country at its most pristine. Haggard's father was a railroad man, and Merle was born in a converted refrigerator car, near the Southern Pacific railroad yard in Bakersfield, California. Today, the most elaborate feature of his moat-enclosed mansion outside Bakersfield is his model electric train set which winds in, out, and around the house.

Haggard's parents had come from Oklahoma, fleeing the Dust Bowl, and in California they became "Okies." Dislocation and the sense of impermanence were his inheritances, and he senses that at heart he is a trainman, for that is an existence all by itself. The brakeman and engineer—and their counterparts the truckers (Haggard wrote and sang the theme song for the television series "Movin' On")—like to keep on the move. It satisfies their restlessness. They might be running from disappointed love, as they are in so many songs, but sometimes you feel that they keep on the move so they won't have to face hopeless ambition.

There is the loneliness of moving, and the isolation, like the loneliness and isolation there had been on the farm and in the mountains. After a while, you embrace that

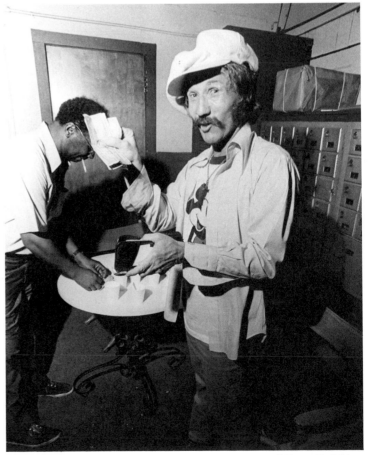

Roy Clark.

Marty Robbins.

145

loneliness and make it speak for freedom and independence.
You hanker for a nice home, a loving wife, your fair share,
kids you can teach to fish, but in the songs it often sounds
as if you love the "hankering" and the "wanting" all by
themselves. As if what you cared about most were the feelings
of pain and loss.

These feelings might make you sad and wistful, but
they don't depress your spirit, for when there are no feelings,
when you are "dead," you get depressed. Being on a train, on a
truck, or just wandering wraps you in isolation, and within
that isolation you feel alive and protected. You are not
confined because you are moving; you are alone and can
create your own sense of yourself without anyone else telling

**Donna Fargo
and country fans.**

you who you are. To be settled and have to suffer lack of a job,
a bad crop, a dirty, small home, demands of others,
demanding kids, cold wives, fickle girls is to deal with
too much killing failure.

In his song, "Mama Tried," Haggard tells that his
father instilled in him the dream of hopping a freight, of
moving without destination. His mother tried to keep a firm
hand on her boy, but after his father's death, when Merle was
nine, he became increasingly rebellious. By fourteen he
had dropped out of school and spent few nights at home.
Flossie Haggard wanted her son to grow up right; she had him
committed to a home for juvenile delinquents to show him
that she meant business. He escaped.

By the time Haggard was eighteen, he had escaped from reform schools numerous times, settled in Eugene, Oregon for a few months, then moved on, returning to Bakersfield and jail. Car thefts, holdups, stealing were his raps. In 1957, he made it to San Quentin, and during one stretch of solitary confinement, the cell next to his was occupied by Caryl Chessman.

When Haggard sings "Branded Man" and "Sing Me Back Home"—songs of prison life when he prayed for death to end his pain—we hear the ache.

The way out for Haggard was music, and he played some in roadhouses, and back in Bakersfield, he worked harder at it. He schooled himself in Jimmie Rodgers, Bob

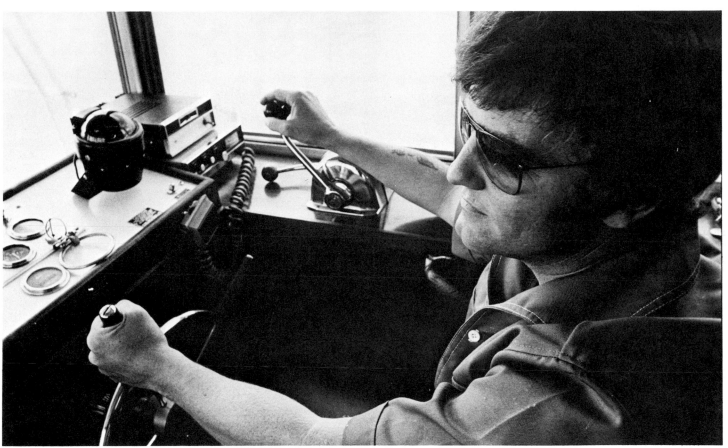

Mickey Newbury.

Wills, Lefty Frizzell.

In the early sixties, Buck Owens was putting Bakersfield on the country-music map, and with Jack McFadden, he formed a booking agency for country performers in the area, including Joe and Rose Maphis, Bonnie Owens (then Buck's wife, later to marry Haggard), Rose Maddox, Freddie Hart, and later on Susan Raye.

Haggard's first big hit was a song by Liz Anderson, "All My Friends Are Gonna Be Strangers" in 1965, but it was his own "Okie from Muskogee" followed by "Fightin' Side of Me" that took him to the top. In Muskogee, so the song says, the college dean is respected, leather boots are worn instead of sandals, white lightning is preferred to LSD, hair is neatly trimmed, they like to pitch woo and hold hands, and Ole Glory is waving at the court house. Obviously, Muskogee is a long way from Bakersfield, and obviously also Haggard knew he was playing with some fantasyland, but the audience took the song as an anthem for the old ways. This isn't the only time a country singer has played to the most simplistic notions of his audience, and with sentiments the artist doesn't share, but the odd thing is that Haggard should have achieved success on two songs that have nothing to do with his most typical work.

His autobiographical songs are wrenched out of real pain and his ballads puncture sentimentality with the realities of joblessness, fear, defeat. His tribute album to Jimmie

Johnny Rodriguez and
Tanya Tucker.

Connie Smith.

Rodgers counts as one of the best, and his appearance as a guest vocalist on Bob Wills's last recordings attests to his ability to understand and re-create country traditions.

Hall, Haggard, and Cash are the three great instances who have found a welcome strength in resisting the blandishments that confused many country performers in seeking a broader audience.

In the country boom, the audience responded most to those performers who matched their idea of what a country star should sound like, thick with regional accent and manners and a lack of sophistication. The new world of country also spurred what is a relatively new phenomenon, the importance of women singers. Though almost to a woman, these

148

singers disclaim the ideals of the feminist movement, all of them have benefited from it and actually foster it. It is less important that the messages of songs like "Stand By Your Man" and "D-I-V-O-R-C-E" seem to place women in a subservient position, for they give a space and dignity to the anxieties of women, and in "I Never Promised You a Rose Garden" and "Harper Valley PTA" there is the raised fist.

Loretta Lynn is the darling of daytime and nighttime interview programs, brought to national attention by the bemused David Frost. He seemed fascinated by this simple country girl who was born in, and sang about, Butcher's Hollow, Kentucky, was a mother at fourteen and a grandmother at twenty-eight. This "Coal Miner's Daughter" is a

Billy Sherrill.

Jeanne Pruett.

self-made woman, and there is a bit of neat playacting in her role as untutored girl.

Merv Griffin, Mike Douglas, Dinah Shore, and Johnny Carson now have an obligation to showcase country performers, and their programs frequently include appearances by Loretta Lynn, Roy Clark, Mel Tillis, Jerry Reed, Melba Montgomery, Buck Owens.

Like Loretta Lynn, Dolly Parton, now with her own syndicated show, makes the audiences do the crossing over. Her big break came when she replaced Norma Jean as the female singer on "The Porter Wagoner Show," and in the few years she has been on her own, she has made a solid reputation for herself. Tammy Wynette was discovered by Billy Sherrill, with whom she wrote most of her hits, and learned phrasing and style from her former husband, George Jones, but she managed to absorb it without blemishing her individuality.

Among the major female singers are those who paved the way for Wynette and Lynn, such as Jan Howard, Skeeter Davis, Jean Shepard, and those who deserve equal celebrity such as Barbara Fairchild ("Teddy Bear Song"), Lynn Anderson, Donna Fargo ("Happiest Girl in the Whole USA"), Bobbie Gentry ("Ode to Billy Joe"), Judy Lynn, Connie Smith, and Barbara Mandrell ("Midnight Oil").

Country's youngsters, Tanya Tucker and Johnny Rodriguez, began as superstars, and they sing as if they had been around forever, for they began with the feeling, in their

Johnny Rodriguez.

songs, that they had seen everything and suffered everything. Tanya Tucker has made a specialty of recording the travails of fallen women, and of their daughters. Rarely has the red light glowed with such a halo, and Rodriguez quickly went from jail (serving a sentence for shooting a deer out of season) to sing at Alamo Village, Texas, where he was heard by Bobby Bare and Tom T. Hall who then provided him with contacts in Nashville.

Charley Pride is country's first major black star (though not the only black performer) that country has produced. To many of his fans, the big surprise is that Pride sings "white," but that kind of clear-cut definition is false, for the breakdown of such categories is the history of American music. A great deal of country music is black based, and black

Bobby Goldsboro.

151

music is no pure-strained tradition either. The musics have been intertwining and cross-fertilizing each other ever since Americans began humming. Pride always speaks reverently of Hank Williams, and Williams was white blues—the style and songs of Pride are no imitations, and if rights are measured out, he probably has the greater right to his style than white performers. In the end, what is amazing is how much alike we all are, how much we share, and for that reason we are compelled to keep on insisting on distinctions, for otherwise we might lose what small sense of individuality we have.

Is the country boom over? Was it all a passing fancy? Did it answer to needs of a specific moment in our history? Have the roots been exhausted, and the recent music robbed

Buck Owens.

of the intensity and freshness of the original? No. Country music is here to stay, and the renegade element in our national character—and in the character of other countries where country music has gained a large following—will keep it alive. Where people constantly insist on their individuality, where they remain dissatisfied with encroachments of government and limitations to freedom, public and private, where there is frustration and the need for expression, country will remain.

No matter that it gets muffled in packaging, more brassy than rugged, more tacky than vital. All that won't last. The impulse to sing, to sing about what you feel and what you experience remains, and the young won't be stilled. There is country tomorrow.

Dolly Parton.

9
Nashville
Tomorrow

Nashville has a long,
respectable history—from eighteenth-century Fort Nashboro
on the serpentine Cumberland River to the 1860s when
the city was the focal point of the Civil War to the present
with its banks and horse farms and maverick politics and
occasional scandals and millionaires and churches everywhere
—a long and thoroughly normal history.

Normal, that is, until the mid-1920s when Clear
Channel WSM beamed across the nation the first Opry
program. It is clear now what the consequences of that first
broadcast were to become. The city has taken on a sort
of crazed, schizophrenic look: churches and normalcy on one
side, Music City on the other, and a barrier as inviolable as
the Great Wall of China between.

Once, the wife of a prominent Nashvillian said to a
visitor: "I hope you won't judge Nashville by the Grand
Ole Opry, but by our symphony." "Madam," he replied,
"there are many fine symphonies, so if I judge Nashville in

that regard, you are in trouble. But there is only one Grand Ole Opry."

That part of Nashville which causes it to be called Music City is like a tough, raw-boned frontier town where anything goes. The façade is raucous and tacky, plastic daubed with colors not found in nature, the total antithesis of the muted browns and greens of the countryside; beer joints; ashtrays and swimming pools shaped like guitars; leather shirts that cost four hundred dollars, hookers in high heels and bobby socks whose attentions cost ten dollars, and singers and pickers who'll play for nothing; rich and poor side by side at the pinball machines in the Merchant's Hotel. The guy in the maroon pants, judging by his custom Continental

Downtown Nashville.

car and the sheer poundage of his turquoise jewelry, has found a gold mine somewhere off in the hills. The fellow next to him will hock his guitar for a bus ticket home. It is all very savage and very real, and there is talent everywhere.

Of course, most don't make it. "Nashville was the roughest," Willie Nelson says in "Me And Paul." Lower Broad Street, down where the Opry used to be, is full of honky tonks with beer-drinking guys who almost made it. They all knew Cash or Kristofferson back when. They all wrote smash hits or played mean guitar, and they all, every one of them, got screwed.

Nashville is like the hard edge of a good country song —it'll cut you. Spirits and lives and fortunes have been destroyed and hundreds of thousands of cumulative hours have been wasted in Nashville. And that is precisely what getting screwed in Nashville is all about: having your precious time wasted.

But Nashville offers one the thrill of happening upon somebody who, some day and with a little luck, you know will be a star; some kid from Indianapolis who gets up at the Exit-In and knocks everybody down with his songs; a girl who sings every night at a beer bar for quarters and truckers' cheers. And I believe that sooner or later, with perseverance and maybe a prayer or two, a good song will be heard and a good voice will get its chance, and life in Nashville, when this happens, can be very pleasant indeed.

Following are quick looks at some Nashville people I feel are going to constitute what Nashville and country music are going to be tomorrow. Of course, the Charley Prides and the Loretta Lynns will be there, too, but these are folks you probably haven't heard of before, so take a close look at the photos because it's my bet you'll be hearing from them very soon. One last thought. These people are only a sample of Nashville's future stars. There are more.

Lana Chapel

She comes from good show-biz stock. Her mother is Jean Chapel, songwriter and guitarist, a most pleasant woman considering how much she's been kicked around. Her father was Salty Holmes, one-time Grand Ole Opry star who quit to go into, you guessed it, aluminum siding. Now Lana confronts the beast.

One hot night a few months ago, she sang me one of her songs, "Almost as Blue as Your Eyes," and I felt as if I were privileged to have a front-row seat to the drama that is Nashville, Tennessee—someone coming from nowhere, anywhere, even from Nashville itself, someone as powerless as this girl, and yet willing to throw her arms around a town without mercy, oblivious of all but her blind love.

Lately, Kris Kristofferson has been producing Lana. I am anxious to see how her devotion will be rewarded.

Rusty Kershaw

He's the other half of the Louisiana Man. He and brother
Doug could have had the world but they let it slip away, Doug
getting lost in his own wild-man Cajun image while he
flailed away on any stage that would have him; Rusty just
wanting to stay happy, get high, play guitar—although there
for a while he got crazy, too, doing too much of everything
that was fun and working too hard at it, eventually winding up
in jail and the funny farm.

But let me tell you what it's like to see Rusty Kershaw
on stage. It's the eyes—sharp, frenzied—that get to you,
flashing the spotlight back at you through tangled strands of
long, black hair. Then, the guitar. Other pickers come
to see him and sit there crying in their beer because they know
they can't touch him. "Awww," he moans, and rolls his
eyes, playing the blues, maybe remembering some dark and
secret backwater of the deep South where you and I have never
been.

Marshall Chapman

She is one of the most beautiful women I know; like some
sleek, wild forest creature when she sings in pain or joy.
I first saw her in a club in Nashville called The Jolly Ox,
where you go to get drunk in an overpriced, phony atmosphere
—or to listen. She was always worth the trouble. Through
songs like "A Woman's Heart Is a Handy Place to Be" and
"Somewhere South of Macon," she'd throw back her lovely
head and wail about broken hearts and lives and times,
bad and good.

The business has stepped on her some, wasted her time,
but that's to be expected. Marshall is very good at what she
does, but even if she weren't, I'd go just to watch her. And
when the time comes, so will you.

Dave Hickey

Born in Fort Worth, Texas, Dave makes Lawrence of Arabia
look plodding and earthbound. A Master of Arts in American
Literature, Dave is a journalist of note and an art critic;
for a time he was editor of *Art In America* and owner of a
gallery. He lives and writes on the Upper East Side of
Manhattan, an isolated lover of country music.

How did Dave Hickey wind up in this book? By
writing songs such as "Cookie and Lila":

Cookie's been to war, and Lila's been to Denver,
And both of them are casualties of someone else's war.*

This song was a hit for Dr. Hook, soon to be cut by other
lights in the business. Other writers don't just like his songs,
they talk about them, so I think Dave is on the verge of getting
famous. Life is okay, and

Death ain't nothin' but a speckled pony
Ain't never been rode.**

* "Cooky and Lila," Baron Every Day Songs, BMI. Quoted with
permission.
** "Speckled Pony," Baron Every Day Songs, BMI. Quoted with
permission.

Bob and Sherry Millsap

In the six and a half years they've been together, they've proven effective an almost Renaissance approach to making a fortune from the music business—that of diversifying rather than concentrating effort in only one of many possible directions. They are doing it all: songwriting and publishing ("Heaven Is My Woman's Love," "She Is My Rock," are Sherry's songs), record production and session playing (Bob is a guitarist), TV production, sound-studio management, advertising, artist management; all this without dependence upon the major labels.

At a time when the large country–music cartels are self-destructing due to the state of the economy, Bob and Sherry are flourishing. Perhaps they, and the few others gutsy and accomplished enough, constitute the vanguard of what the record business will have to become in order to survive honestly and with grace.

Sharon Thompson

Sharon was seventeen, from Windsor, North Carolina, and had never been in a bar before, so lower Broad Street in Nashville, with its arcade feel, must have looked to her like something out of sin city. The first bar she went into turned out to be the Music City Lounge (Cecil Petty, prop.), a benevolent, if raucous, home where she nightly trained her pure country voice. The pickup bands and the truckers and the tourists came and went, but now, "I wouldn't leave my forty-four-year-old," she says with a smile for Cecil, "for nothing."

She has received attention from magazine writers and has appeared on a TV documentary (NBC's "Weekend"), but her only records so far have been on the small, almost distributionless Americountry label. Sharon is "hard country, *hard*. Yeah, I listened to pop music when I was a kid, but you know, all little kids do that."

Jim Varney

Funnyman from Lexington, Kentucky, Jim is the English-Irish son of a hobo/miner/cowboy/boxer. He tells stories—acts them out—onstage before Cash or Dr. Hook or whoever you've paid to see comes out. I suppose that makes him a comedian, although there is more to it than that. There is theater too—raw humor that is as much a part of the tradition as Jerry Clower's Marcel Ledbetter or John Henry Faulk's Pea-vine.

Via the Barter Theater and various clubs in New York, Jim went to Nashville to work at Opryland, and he made a name for himself on local TV where, as tough-ass Marine Sergeant Glory, he shilled dairy products. While there, he lived in an apartment below a massage parlor, played the Exit-In and pinball machines, made friends and not much money—at the same time polishing his act. He has recently moved to California.

Jim Rushing

He writes fine, soulful songs like Charley Pride's hit, "I Hope You're Feelin' Me Like I'm Feelin' You." Lubbock-born, Jim found himself in college not having very much fun, and thereafter, was unswerving in his intent to dissociate himself from all grim pursuits.

And songwriting, too, at its best, is fun. But "deep suspicion" is the dark glass through which he views the power structure of the music business, the white-vinyl-boot-clad men who hold his career suspended like an egg above the hard streets of Nashville. But Jim Rushing is a thorough pro and will make it in spite of all this.

Guy Clark

Guy might be just like any of those long, tall, drawly types from Texas trying to look and sound like Jerry Jeff Walker if there were anything at all mediocre about him. But there isn't. Hell, the same goes for his woman (that's Susanna sitting beside him there, all smiles). Guy already enjoys a healthy reputation as a songwriter—"L.A. Freeway" and "Desperados Waiting For the Train" have been cut by who knows how many people—and, his first album, *Old No. 1*, is out on the RCA label and seems to be going places. So maybe in a few years, there'll be a bunch of Texas types lolling about trying hard to look like Guy Clark: you know, quoting his songs and all, and praying hard, "Please, God, send me a woman looks like Susanna."

Louisa Cook

Am I a princess in disguise,
Am I a Cinderella child?
Someplace there's got to be
A better place for me.*

The words are from "Geneva," a song of Louisa's just recently
cut by new ABC-Dot artist, Jeris Ross, also the first thing
Louisa's ever had recorded. Tender lyrics from a tender
woman—tender without being weak. Ever since she first set
foot in Nashville, she's known what she's wanted; the
only problem has been how to find it, the business being
what it is, and songwriters, especially women, being fair game
for everybody with a Cadillac and a fast mouth.

Louisa's starting all over again now, after performing
and writing in Northern California for a few years. The
signs are all good so far, and I'd be willing to bet she makes
it, on her own, without compromise.

* Quoted with permission, Screen Gems/Columbia Music, BMI.

Chris Le Doux

Chris and Peggy and three-year-old Clay call Kaycee, Wyoming, home, but more often than not they are adding miles to the three hundred thousand their van, Rodeo Rose, has already logged. All so Chris can log a few miles and lot of bruises on bucking horses for love, money, and the just plain hell of it. Ever since he was fourteen and the Little Britches world champ at bareback bronco busting, Chris has been working the rodeos, making enough of a name for himself to rank among the top fifteen cowboys in the world five years out of the six he's been a pro.

He sings a mighty fine song, too, five albums worth, and all for American Cowboy Songs, Inc., an entirely family-owned-and-run operation. The songs, many of which are Chris's own, are genuine; the production is good; and you'll be pleased to know that Chris shouldn't be hard to find since rodeo is catching on these days.

Byron Warner

A few years ago, Byron, his sister, and another fellow had a big hit called "In the Morning," and for a while, everything looked like roses. But something soured, and since then, he's been through about seven different kinds of hell, the only bright spot being Cynthia Ann Beckham of South Carolina, now Mrs. Warner.

Byron is a brand new father, a disc jockey, a storyteller, one of Nashville's finest TV and radio actors, and a good friend of mine. His curse has been that he isn't devious enough to get in there and wade with the sharks.

He is also a great songwriter and singer—not good, great. One day, his talents are going to make somebody very wealthy. I only hope that somebody is Byron Warner.

Selected Bibliography

Anderson, Patrick. "The Real Nashville." *The New York Times Magazine*, August 31, 1975, p. 10.

Bart, Teddy. *Inside Music City, U.S.A.* Nashville: Aurora Publishers, 1970.

Broderick, Richard, ed. *The New York Times 100 Great Country Songs.* New York: Quadrangle/The New York Times Book Co., 1973.

Cash, W. J. *The Mind of the South.* New York: Vintage Books/Random House, 1941.

Combs, Josiah H. *Folk-Songs of the Southern United States.* Edited by D. K. Wilgus. Published for the American Folklore Society. Austin and London: The University of Texas Press, 1967.

Cook, Bruce. *Listen to the Blues.* New York: Charles Scribner's Sons, 1973.

Danker, Frederick E. "The Repertory and Style of a Country Singer." *Journal of American Folklore* 338 (1974): 310–329.

Danker, Frederick E. "Country Music." *Yale Review*, Spring, 1974, pp. 392–404.

Gentry, Linnell. *A History and Encyclopedia of Country, Western, and Gospel Music.* 2nd ed. Nashville: Clairmont Corporation, 1969.

Green, Archie. *Only a Miner.* Urbana: University of Illinois Press, 1972.

Keillor, Garrison. "At the Opry." *The New Yorker*, May 6, 1974, pp. 46–70.

Koon, William Henry. "Newgrass, Oldgrass and Bluegrass." *JEMF Quarterly*, vol. 10, part 1 (Spring 1974): 15–18. University of California at Los Angeles, The John Edwards Memorial Foundation.

Lydon, Michael. *Rock Folk.* New York: The Dial Press, 1971.

Malone, Bill C. *Country Music U.S.A. A Fifty-year History.* Published for the American Folklore Society. Memoir Series, General Editor: John Greenway. Austin and London: The University of Texas Press, 1968.

Pleasants, Henry. *The Great American Popular Singers.* New

York: Simon & Schuster, 1974.

Rooney, James. *Bossmen: Bill Monroe and Muddy Waters.*
New York: The Dial Press, 1971.

Rosenberg, Neil V. "From Sound to Style: The Emergence
of Bluegrass." *Journal of American Folklore*, 80 (1967):
143–150.

Shelton, Robert. *The Country Music Story: A Picture History
of Country and Western Music.* Photos by Burt Goldblatt.
Secaucus, N.J.: Castle Books, 1966.

Shestack, Melvin. *The Encyclopedia of Country Music.* New
York: Thomas Y. Crowell, 1974.

Smith, L. Mayne. "An Introduction to Bluegrass." *Journal of
American Folklore* 38 (1965): 245–256.

Stambler, Irwin, and Landon, Grelun. *Golden Guitars: The
Story of Country Music.* New York: Four Winds Press, 1971.

Williams, Roger M. *Sing a Sad Song: The Life of Hank
Williams.* Garden City, N.Y.: Doubleday & Co., 1970.

Townsend, Charles R. *San Antonio Rose: The Life and Music
of Bob Wills.* Music In American Life Series. Urbana:
University of Illinois Press, 1976.

Wren, Christopher S. *Winners Got Scars Too: The Life and
Legends of Johnny Cash.* New York: The Dial Press, 1971.

Index